F...

Brittany

Jarrold Publishing

CONTENTS

Title page: Lobster-pots

Morgat

Introducing Brittany

France offers no more enduring experience to the traveller than a visit to Brittany. The distinctive granite peninsula, so different from other parts of the country, leaves its own unique and incomparable impression. The Ancients, who conceived of the world as a flat disc and referred to its extremities as 'Finis Terrae', found their land's end here in the west of Brittany, the furthermost corner-stone of Europe, where the sun sinks into the sea. It was from here, they believed, that the souls of the dead set sail in little boats, to follow their god into the afterlife. Today the westernmost *département* of Brittany still bears the name 'Finistère'.

What then awaits the visitor to this part of France, with its striking blend of land and sea? Capricious weather certainly, a land of changeable winds where no two days are ever alike and where there is a constant atmospheric interplay of blues and greys – in the middle of a rain shower the clouds will suddenly open to release the sun. The weather here is in continuous flux; it is never really settled – but there are no real extremes either.

Armor – the Breton coast

Over and over again Brittany reveals its geographical diversity. To begin with there is Armor – a Breton name meaning 'land by the sea' – the coastal strip more than 2,000 km in length, its granite fringes perpetually gnawed and attacked by the sea. Bays, gulfs, tongues of land, islands and islets, cliffs and river estuaries follow one after another, while picturesque fishing villages nestle alongside fashionable seaside resorts. Sometimes, smooth and with a sparkling play of light, the sea will resemble a dazzling sheet of silver foil, only to turn rough once more and stormy grey, frothing angrily with all Neptune's wrath. The breakers ravage the very substance of the peninsula, leaving behind stupendous formations in the rock. Never will one's skin have felt more invigorated than here, after a walk by the sea when the salt and iodine spray flies from the wave crests breaking against the rocky cliffs.

Here too is a seemingly endless sequence of long, white sandy beaches, dotted with dunes. The beaches are among the most alluring of summer's delights, places where, whether by taking to some kind of sport, gathering shells or catching shrimps, the city-dweller can rediscover the pleasure to be found in simple things. Again and again he will also fall under the unforgettable spell cast by the spectacle of the tides, for nowhere on earth is there a greater difference between high water and low. As a result there are extensive 'amphibious' areas which invite exploration, and many a small island can often be reached on foot. A whiff of slippery seaweed and mud hangs over these tidal flats, where small boats and fishing smacks lie fast aground, their empty hulls tilting to one side. At St-Malo the tidal barrage stands as a symbol of environmentally friendly energy production (see page 37), just as deserving of the visitor's attention as the beds of cultivated mussels and oysters whose secrets the sea reveals only at low water. These seafood delicacies are harvested along the north coast from Cancale, and on the south coast from Bélon near Quimperlé as far as Camaret and St-Nazaire (see pages 36–37).

Armor – the Quiberon Peninsula

The coast of Brittany though has yet another face, being in many places extremely dangerous. It is said that the Bretons are born sailors, their hearts lapped by the waves. The sight of so many little fishermen's chapels by the sea, however, makes you wonder how many anxious women and girls have prayed over the centuries for the safe return of their menfolk – husbands and fathers, brothers and sons. The waters of Brittany in fact are just as notorious as those of Cape Horn. Here innumerable ships have foundered on the rocks in poor visibility and severe storms, the inhabitants of the coast readily seizing upon the wreckage. Here too countless

Argoat landscape

bodies of the anonymous ship-wrecked have been washed up on the shore. Today the coast is guarded by a multitude of lights, many of considerable range. Yet accidents at sea can still not be ruled out – one has only to recall the spring of 1978 and the catastrophe involving the oil tanker *Amoco Cadiz* which caused such devastating pollution.

Argoat – cultivated hinterland with islands of forest
There is also quite another side to Brittany, this time away from the coast – the Argoat, 'land of woods' and land of farmers. Here the once extensive forests of the Middle Ages have long since given way to agriculture, shrinking to a few islands of woodland. The countryside of this inland part of Brittany is predominantly green, a region of pastoral peacefulness. Before you lies a labyrinth of hedges, with a scattering of hamlets and villages or little towns, and tranquil parishes dominated by ornate belfries – all enveloped in fertile arable land.

From the few remaining vestiges of forest it is still possible to picture the earlier enchanted woodlands of the Celtic sagas and legends (see page 16). Refreshing streams wind under the high canopy of greenery. In areas where the land remains uncultivated there stretches a heathland of tough grasses peppered with stunted pines and juniper-bushes, and chaotically piled boulders. Here the broom flowers a flaming yellow in spring, and autumn is a blaze of violet heather. These areas are also interspersed with swamps and gloomy bog lakes, the best known of which is *Yeun Elez.*

It is in this heathland that one comes across those massive and enigmatic monuments in stone, dating back to megalithic prehistory and shrouded in legend. Best known is the 'army of stone' at Carnac, an extraordinary collection of menhirs the origin and significance of which remain a puzzle to the present day (see pages 51–52).

In the sleepy villages and hamlets of this harsh landscape the houses are of grey granite. They are plain, almost humble, with hydrangea bushes, geraniums and fuchsias their only decoration. Here you will meet folk whose character bears the unmistakable stamp of their Celtic heritage. They are a deeply pious people, committed Catholics yet at the same time adhering to saints not authorised by any pope, and in fact heathen in their origins.

Breton culture emerged as the loser from confrontation with first the Romans and later the French. Along with this subjugation came suppression of the Breton tongue, a language deriving from Celtic. Although Brittany has now belonged to France for about 470 years the Breton longing for independence still persists, and from time to time has developed into active separatism and sometimes bloody exchanges with the representatives of central government in Paris. The old frontier towns with their fortifications, such as Fougères, Vitré and Châteaubriant, testify only too clearly to these long-continuing tensions between Brittany and France.

The modern face of Brittany

Ever since being incorporated into France in 1532 Brittany has been one of her problem children, and until well into the 20th c. economic development passed the region by. The result was large-scale migration to other parts of the country and into the cities. In spite of this, because of a high birth-rate the population continues to remain steady even today, and Brittany is consequently one of France's most densely populated regions, at least in the coastal areas. Since – despite a considerable decline in numbers – about a quarter of all employment is still accounted for by agriculture, and since fishing continues to head the list of livelihoods here in contrast to other coastal regions of France, a process of expansion and intensification could yet close the economic gap between Brittany and the rest of France.

Definitely in need of correction, though, is the all too common idea of a poor Brittany which is still isolated and primitive. The region today is completely integrated into modern France. Fast four-lane roads encircle the peninsula, and almost every minor road is surfaced. On the outskirts of big towns and cities such as Rennes, Nantes, Brest and Lorient whole new districts with big shopping centres have grown up, and large industrial plants have been established. Major technical projects, such as the tidal power station in the Rance estuary, the Centre of Space Communications in Pleumeur-Bodou, the Brennilis nuclear power station (shut down in 1987), the fishing harbour at Lorient-Keroman, the French oceanographic research institute in Brest, the institute of marine biology in Roscoff, the large shipyards at Nantes and St-Nazaire and the Citroën car factory at Rennes, have all helped bring Brittany firmly into the 20th century.

Essential details in brief

Brittany: French name *Bretagne*; Celtic name *Armorica*; Breton name *Breiz(h)*.

Area: The peninsula of north-west France jutting out into the Atlantic Ocean covers some 27,208 sq km, about 5% of the total area of France. It is about 250 km long and from 100 to 150 km across.

Administrative divisions: The Brittany *région* is made up of four *départements*: *Ille-et-Vilaine* (chief town: Rennes), *Côtes-du-Nord* (chief town: St-Brieuc), *Morbihan* (chief town: Vannes) and *Finistère* (chief town: Quimper). Historically Brittany used also to include the department of Loire-Atlantique (chief town: Nantes), which since 1964 has been part of the Pays de la Loire.

Population: 2.78 million, 5% of the total population of France. Population density: 102 inhabitants per sq km, exactly the same as the average for the rest of France. There are big differences between the coastal zone, with its large towns, and the interior which is experiencing a continuing exodus from the countryside. In the interior, agricultural holdings are too small and insufficiently equipped with modern machinery to be competitive in the European market. Population growth: despite high levels of migration, population density remains steady owing to the high birth-rate.

Highest elevations: *Roc Trévezel* and *Signal de Toussaines*, both 384 m and both part of the Monts d'Arrée chain, the remains of a once mighty Palaeozoic mountain range.

Length of coast: 1,200 km (or 2,500 km counting all the gulfs and bays).

Tides: The tidal range experienced on the north coast of Brittany in particular is greater than anywhere else in the world. In the bay of Mont-St-Michel the difference in height between high and low water is some 14 m and at low water the sea recedes 18 km from the shore. On the flood it is not only the estuaries and river valleys that fill with seawater; even levels in the large bays, like the Rade (roadstead) de Brest and the Golfe du Morbihan, are affected.

Historic frontiers: Fougères, Vitré, Châteaubriant, Ancenis and Clisson are all strongholds by means of which one can trace the former frontier of Brittany.

Signposts of history

Before 4000 BC: Traces of settlement from the Palaeolithic and Mesolithic Ages.

4000–2000 BC: During the Neolithic period the area is a centre of megalithic culture (dolmens, menhirs, alignments, cromlechs and artefacts).

2000–500 BC: Copper and Bronze Ages (carved menhirs, late megalithic tombs, ceramics, axes, jewellery).

Around 500 BC: Beginning of the Iron Age. Migration of the Celtic tribes.

58–56 BC: Caesar subdues the Veneti in the Golfe du Morbihan; process of Romanisation begins.

Armorica becomes Brittany

27 BC: Part of the Roman province of Lugdunensis.

5th c. AD: Migration of Celtic tribes from Britain fleeing from the Angles and Saxons. They settle in Brittany, bringing their language and Christianity.

579: Waroch's victory over the Gallo-Romans in Vannes.

Around 600: Gradlon's Breton kingdom in Cornwall.

799: Morvan, King of Brittany, makes tribute payments to Louis I (the Pious). Although Louis defeats him the people continue to rebel.

The independent Duchy of Brittany

826: Louis I makes Nominoë Duke of Brittany.

846: Nominoë routs Frankish troops at Redon, following which Charles the Bald acknowledges the autonomy of Brittany.

851: Breton troops are victorious at Le Grand-Fougeray. Charles the Bald recognises Nominoë's son Erispoë as King of Brittany. Erispoë acquires the areas around Rennes, Nantes and Retz.

857–874: Breton territory is extended to include Anjou, the Cotentin and Avrachin.

933: Following invasion by the Normans (Norsemen), the Bretons lose the Cotentin and the islands of Guernsey and Jersey.

952–990: Period of Norman domination.

1113: Brittany is a fiefdom of England.

1166: The Plantagenet king of England, Henry II, controls Brittany.

1213: The Duchy of Brittany passes to Pierre Mauclerc of the House of Dreux. Ducal power is enhanced under Pierre and his son Jean le Roux. They maintain their independence against the King of France.

1341–1365: Breton War of Succession: the dukes of the House of Montfort rule Brittany. The Hundred Years War between England and France is in progress (lasting until 1453). The Bretons side mainly with the English and Burgundians. The arts flourish.

Brittany becomes part of France

1491: Anne de Bretagne marries Charles VIII though remaining Duchess of Brittany.

1499: After the death of Charles VIII Anne de Bretagne marries Louis XII and again becomes Queen of France.

1514: Anne de Bretagne dies. Her daughter Claude marries the future François I of France.

1532: Brittany finally becomes part of France when, under pressure from her husband, Claude cedes the Duchy to the French Crown.

1550–1650: The cloth trade in Brittany prospers. The Breton parishes emerge.

1598: The Wars of Religion between Catholics and Huguenots are brought to an end by the Edict of Nantes.

1685: Louis XIV revokes the Edict. With the departure of the Huguenots from Brittany the cloth-making industry starts to decline.

1764: The Breton parliament opposes Louis XV – an early sign of the impending French Revolution.

1789: The Bretons, enthusiastic supporters of the Revolution, hope for a revival of regionalism. However, the autonomy in fiscal, legal and military affairs originally granted in 1532 is set aside, and Brittany is divided into five departments: the four of which it still consists today, plus Loire-Atlantique. Only the Supreme Court in Rennes remains as a wholly Breton authority.

1940–44/45: The Breton independence movement is encouraged by the Germans. As a consequence, following liberation many supporters of Breton autonomy are regarded as collaborators and separatists.

1957: Militant movements call for the 'liberation of Brittany'. Their aim is a revival of the language and culture of the region.

1964: Brittany with Rennes the chief town is designated an economic region, though minus Nantes and the department of Loire-Atlantique.

1974: Associations supporting the Breton independence movement are banned, but some Bretons still remain active 'underground'.

1978: A Brittany council is formed charged with reviving the region's ancient cultural heritage.

Carnac

Menhir at St-Duzec

Megalithic monuments in Brittany

In the Neolithic period (New Stone Age) between 4000 and 2000 BC, peoples presumed to have originated in Asia arrived in the area, having migrated westwards in search of the place where the sun they worshipped set. They were responsible for the construction of countless megalithic monuments. Such monuments are found in many coastal areas, including Malta, Sardinia, Corsica and the Orkneys, but are especially numerous here in Brittany. The term megalith (Greek: megas = big, lithos = stone) refers to various different types of monument formed out of large stones.

Even today the precise reasons for building such huge structures remain a mystery; it has proved impossible to reach any truly definitive conclusion as to whether they served a scientific, political or religious purpose. What does seem clear though is that these monuments, scattered over the whole area in vast numbers, were associated in some way with a death cult and worship of a Mother Goddess.

Menhirs — standing stones of disputed purpose

Of all the megaliths the menhirs are the most remarkable. The name derives from the Breton word meaning 'long stone' (men = stone, hir = long) and refers to single upright standing stones. Where these are set in several straight rows running alongside one another they are called *alignments*. Although such alignments are found in other parts of Europe, such as Corsica, those in Brittany are the most impressive as well as the most numerous, especially around Carnac. The menhirs are variously interpreted as thrones for the soul, fertility symbols or memorial stones. Now lying on the ground broken into four pieces, the 'Grand Menhir' or Men-er-Hroëc'h at *Locmariaquer*, 350 tonnes in weight and at 20.3 m the longest of the menhirs, is regarded by some archaeologists as the centre-piece of a great observatory, while others see it as a navigational mark for mariners entering the Golfe du Morbihan. The tallest menhir still standing in Brittany (Kerloas near Plouarzel, Finistère) measures some 12 m. Exactly how these massive monoliths were quarried and how they were transported and set upright is explained graphically in the Museum of Prehistory at Carnac (see page 52).

The specific arrangement of the alignments probably reflects some cult practice, perhaps forming a kind of processional route. Often they terminate with a diagonal line behind which stands a half circle of menhirs – the *cromlech* (Celtic: kramon = curve, lech = place, stone). In some cases it is possible from the layout of the menhirs to recognise a rectangular ground-plan, such configurations being known as 'quadrilatères', stone squares. Around Carnac alone there are twelve alignments and fourteen stone circles, cromlechs, etc., of which the most important are Le Ménec, Kermario and Kerlescan. In Finistère, the most westerly coastal department, there are in all twelve alignments and seventeen stone circles, etc., extant.

Tombs beneath earth mounds

Dolmens (Breton: dol = table, men = stone) are a form of burial practised by the Neolithic inhabitants of Brittany. They consist of a chamber made from four to six vertical stones supporting one or two stone roof-slabs. Originally all the dolmens were beneath mounds of earth, so the term 'stone table' probably only came into use when the stones were revealed following natural erosion of the earth covering.

In Brittany there are examples not only of the simplest type of dolmen but also of the dolmen 'à galerie' or 'à couloir' (gallery grave), the dolmen 'à cabinet' or 'à chambre latérale' (gallery grave with side chamber), the dolmen 'à grand dallage' (paved dolmen) and the dolmen 'à encorbellement' (tholos with the so-called false vaulting). Whereas in a gallery tomb the passage is clearly distinguishable in the ground-plan from the burial chamber, in an 'allée couverte' (long grave) there is only one elongated space, created by parallel upright stones and the roof-slabs placed over them. The uprights often have engravings such as depictions of the goddess, fertility symbols, axes and crooks.

The word *tumulus* properly refers to earth mounds covering the dolmens. As well as tumuli there are mounds of rough stones known as *cairns* (e.g. at Barnenez and Gavrinis). These terms tend however to be used inaccurately: the St-Michel Tumulus in Carnac, for instance, has a covering of stones as well as an earth layer. In addition to a central grave most sites usually contain smaller chambered graves, or dolmens of various dates; in consequence they are also known as necropolises (cemeteries). Grave-goods including axe-blades, daggers with flint blades, chains and ceramics have been unearthed and are now exhibited in the museums of prehistory at Carnac and Vannes.

The densest concentration of dolmens, menhirs and alignments is found in Morbihan and especially in the Golfe de Carnac. Two sites are of particular interest: the St-Michel Tumulus in Carnac, the largest burial mound in Europe; and the royal sepulchre at Gavrinis, one of the loveliest grave-monuments anywhere, situated on an uninhabited island in the gulf.

✝ Churches and calvaries

Between the 15th and the mid-17th c., art and architecture in Brittany took a highly original turn in the form of the parish close or holy ground with its distinctive calvary. This form of religious folk art is entirely unique to Brittany and any visitor should certainly make a point of seeing at least some examples (see pages 71–73 for details of a round tour of parish closes).

Typically the walled close is reached through a triumphal archway intended to concentrate the mind on death. Beyond the steps to the entrance the visitor must overcome an obstacle, usually a wall of stone slabs set into the gate. Within the close itself cluster the church, calvary and charnel-house or ossuary.

Architectural testaments to Breton piety

Brittany, a strictly Catholic region, is full of churches. There are nine cathedrals alone, the most famous of which are St-Pol-de-Léon, Quimper, Nantes, Tréguier and Dol-de-Bretagne. Then there are the thousands of rural churches and chapels, often worth visiting on account of their originality. But twenty churches in particular are especially worth seeing for their architecture and furnishings.

In the 11th and 12th c., churches were built in the Romanesque style. Brittany has relatively few, as it was extremely weak economically at that time. Examples are found at Redon, Daoulas, Loctudy and St-Gildas-de-Rhuys, in addition to the curious circular temple at Lanleff.

Until the second half of the 12th c. Breton master builders were largely sub-

Quimper Cathedral

servient to Norman influences. They then began to follow their own Early Gothic direction whereby, by increasing the size of windows, they were able to flood the choir and aisles with light while leaving the central nave immersed in semi-darkness. The church of Notre-Dame-de-Roscudon in Pont-Croix is a good example of this innovation, showing clearly at the same time how the weightiness of earlier centuries had been overcome. In the 16th and 17th c. a thriving cloth trade and accompanying affluence brought about a keen rivalry between Brittany's small towns. As a result the dimensions of many a church built during this period seem quite out of proportion to the size of the town.

Like their Romanesque predecessors Brittany's large Gothic cathedrals and churches still bear the unmistakable imprint of Norman influence, seen for example in the tall naves of the cathedrals of St-Pol-de-Léon and Dol-de-Bretagne. Their magnificent ribbed vaulting, however, stands in contrast to the barrel-vaults usual elsewhere. The architecture of the Late Gothic churches is in the Flamboyant style (*flamboyant*, flaming, is France's own art-historical term for Late Gothic in its peculiarly French manifestation – the upper sections of the tracery being elongated and thus interpreted as flames). In many cases vagaries of finance meant that building work had to be extended over several centuries, so the development of the Gothic style can often be followed from beginning to end in these churches. Renaissance additions such as belfries (Pleyben and Dirinon for example) or porches (Landerneau) are also frequently to be seen.

Typical features of Breton churches

The Bretons attached great importance to their belfries – 15th c. Gothic towers over the transept, with pointed spires and pierced bell galleries, Renaissance-style towers decorated with timberwork and arcades, and lighter towers or galleries of bells above the west front. The most famous of all Breton towers is the 77-m-high 'Kreisker' lantern tower on the chapel of the same name at St-Pol-de-Léon. Vauban, the celebrated military architect who died in 1707, considered it a marvel of balance and boldness.

The porches, always built on the south side of a church, were creations of the Gothic and Renaissance periods and provided a place for persons of importance to gather. Figures of the Apostles decorate the niches above the stone benches on either side of the entrance to the church.

Between the 15th and 18th c. the churches were furnished with splendid galleries, pulpits, altars, fonts, stone and wood carvings, choir-stalls and organs. Carved beams – often with grotesque reliefs, some painted, some not – are found in the naves (La Martyre and Pleyben for example). Running round the nave these friezes hide the join between the stone wall and the timber vaulting. Rood-beams (at Lampaul-Guimiliau for instance) are carved beams anchored into the walls of the church and spanning the width of the nave without further support; they are often adorned with a crucifixion group. They serve the same purpose as a rood-screen. The latter, inexhaustibly rich in ornamental carvings, occupies the position from where prayers and the gospels are read. Most are painted and the carving is as delicate as lacework (there is a particularly beautiful example at St-Fiacre near Le Faouët). By way of exception the Flamboyant-style rood-screen in the church at Le Folgoët is not of wood but of carved pink granite, and is especially elegant.

Because of Brittany's damp climate, frescos are rarely to be found in Breton churches. Important though are the Dance of Death frescos at Kermaria-an-Isquit and Kernascléden. Some churches also have fine paintings on glass; the windows in the chapel of Notre-Dame-du-Crann in Spézet and the churches of St-Fiacre near Le Faouët and La Roche-Maurice are particularly good examples.

Ossuaries were used to house skulls and bones which, owing to lack of space in the cemetery, had to be dug up again long after burial. Fountains dedicated to one or other of the saints and decorated with ornate gables are often found near chapels and pilgrim churches.

The Passion rendered in stone: the calvaries

The calvaries (*calvaires*) are a unique and exceptionally attractive feature of the Breton parish close. Representing Golgotha, they originated in the Renaissance, the oldest at Tronoën dating from the end of the 15th c., the most recent from the end of the 17th or early 18th c. They are carved with numerous granite figures, often archaically squat, of a crude simplicity and usually touchingly naïve. These stand on an altar-like base crowned by a tall stone cross. Although wind and weather have blurred the features on some of the faces, no visitor can fail to be moved by them. The Breton sculptors were inspired by the 15th c. Passion and mystery plays which were so popular at the time, and as a result curious and even comic figures can often be discovered set alongside scenes from the life and Passion of Christ. The often rough craftsmanship of these lay artists and the hardness of the granite with which they worked account only in part for the limited realism with which individual figures are depicted; a kind of stylistic canon or unwritten rule required that the human form and gestures be represented in a certain fashion the length and breadth of Brittany. The best-known calvaries are those at Guimiliau (with 200 figures), St-Thégonnec, Plougastel-Daoulas, Pleyben and Tronoën.

Paul Gauguin (1848–1903), proponent of primitivism and Symbolism in painting, found positive inspiration for his work in the rustic art of the calvaries. He forsook the sophistication of Paris where he was living at the time to experience for himself the simple Breton way of life and to capture it on his canvases, painting here at the 'world's end' in this landscape of few shapes, in the peculiarly Breton light which bestows such vitality on outlines and colours.

Brittany's 7,777 saints

According to a local saying there are seven thousand, seven hundred and seventy-seven saints – no matter if by far the greater number of them have never been recognised by any pope. The Bretons have appointed a saint for every circumstance of life: for their animals, for the sick, for lovers, and even for boredom. Every little town has its own patron saint, and wayside shrines, stelae, chapels and churches are to be found everywhere dedicated to them. After the coming of the Celtic Christians to Brittany seven bishoprics were created. Their bishops were also the first Breton saints: Samson, Malo, Brieuc, Tugdual, Pol the Aurelian, Corentin and Patern. St Yves (1253–1303), about whom quite a lot is known from historical sources, became the most widely acclaimed saint of all. Patron saint of judges and advocates, he was canonised just forty years after his death. His reputation for incorruptibility, for the justice of his judgements and for his championing of the weak extended far beyond the bounds of Brittany.

Every year, at places throughout Brittany, pilgrimages known as *pardons* take place in honour of the saints (the name deriving from the ceremonies in which pilgrims are forgiven their sins). Although in earlier times each parish would celebrate its own pardon, today only about sixty are held. The menfolk, dressed in regional costume and bearing reliquaries and banners, make a long penitential procession along the route, biniou- (bagpipe) and bombarde-players at their head. The best-known pardons are those held at Ste-Anne-la-Palud, Tréguier, Locronan and Ste-Anne-d'Auray.

Festivals: lace head-dresses and Celtic music

During the summer months there are festivals in many Breton towns and villages; they present a good opportunity to enjoy the sight of people in their regional costume. Eye-catching and everywhere different are the women's lace head-dresses. The Bigouden *coiffe* is the most remarkable of all; it is hard to imagine how this lace structure, about 50 cm high and not unlike a unicorn's horn, can survive on a windy day (see page 62). The atmosphere is all very informal and everyone who wants to is welcome to join in the folk-dancing, to the accompaniment of traditional Celtic instruments – bombarde, biniou, harp and drum. The Celtic harp has now become more widely known once again through the work of the Breton singer Alain Stivell, and today, together with the Celtic gift for poetry, is the very embodiment of Breton cultural identity. Well-known dances include the *Sabotée* – performed by the womenfolk as the men crack their whips – and the *Jabadato*, danced at weddings. In days gone by the *Piller-Lann* was the only dance tolerated by the bishops since it involved no physical contact between the performers. Naturally the well-being of all the merrymakers is more than taken care of at these festivals, with pancakes, snacks and cider. Among the larger-scale musical events are the Cornouaille festival in Quimper, the Inter-Celtic festival in Lorient and the bagpipe festival in Brest.

Land of legends

The name of one stretch of the coast in the vicinity of Le Folgoët – the *Côte des Légendes* – demonstrates just how important myths and legends are in Brittany. The Breton myths all have their sources in the common corpus of ideas and religious beliefs held by the Celts and their priests, the Druids – they are myths born of heathen religion interwoven with historical fact and Christianity. Mist and howling storms; monsters sculpted naturally in stone; wave-pounded, foam-spattered cliffs and caves bearing the names of the Devil and Hell; at Carnac a veritable petrified army of stone; a heathland streaked with wisps of fog – the landscape alone evokes that other world of legends and fairytales. These tell of how the fairy Vivien bewitched the magician Merlin in the Forest of Brocéliande; of Tristan and Isolde, protagonists in the classic medieval love story; and of the legendary knight Bluebeard and the prophesy of his death by the hand of his son.

When Neptune, God of the Sea, makes his reign of terror felt through icy floods, tempestuous winds and seething, turbulent waves, the Breton soul is ill at ease. Out of fear of the unfathomable, the imagination fashions awful things...

Ys – city beneath the waves

Beneath the sea in the Bay of Douarnenez, so it is said, lies the Breton Sodom, the sunken city of Ys, a once renowned and beautiful city ruled over by the wise and good King Gradlon, and in the 6th c. the capital of the old county of Cornouaille. Gradlon had built mighty dykes to protect Ys against the huge spring tides which flooded into the bay, and himself kept guard over the key to the great sluice-gates.

But the wealth of the city made the inhabitants sinful and godless, the King's own daughter Dahut most of all. She it was who fell into lustful liaison with the Devil and stole the sluice-key from her father's care. Out of curiosity she opened the gates, whereupon waves as tall as houses swept through the streets and alleyways dragging animals, people and buildings into the sea. King Gradlon had time only to swing himself and his daughter into the saddle and ride for safety from the flood. But soon the pair proved too heavy for his horse and it was then that St Guénolé ordered the King to throw down the Devil's mistress. Gradlon's heart was sorely tried, for he had suspected nothing of his daughter's sinful life, and so it was St Guénolé himself who pushed Dahut into the water. At once the sea became smooth. King Gradlon rode on and chose Quimper as his new capital, leaving Ys, the once beautiful royal city, submerged beneath the waves. Now, it is said, on nights when the sea is calm, the bells of the church tower of Ys can still be heard pealing out their warning. And Dahut, in the guise of the wicked fairy Morgan, still lures fishermen and sailors into peril.

Asterix and Obelix, two Bretons known the world over

Asterix and Obelix, one a little fellow, the other a giant of a man, are two Bretons known today all over the world. For numerous nations are familiar with this comic strip set in the world of Gallo-Roman Antiquity. These colourful cartoons (with speech bubbles sometimes including Latin phrases) were the creation of the late

Right: Typical Brittany coastline

René Goscinny and illustrator Alberto Uderzo. The series, which since 1959 has appeared in its millions in a host of languages and has even been produced in a Latin version, pokes fun at the engaging and amusing foibles of the French, and at the French style of patriotism.

The rest of Gaul having been occupied by the Romans there remains only a single pocket of Gallic resistance, in the far north-west of the country, in Brittany. Here lives the hero of the series, the indomitable Asterix. This little man acquires the strength of a bear when he drinks the Druid Miraculix's magic potion. His friend Obelix, fat and good-natured, makes the menhir-shaped boulders use as missiles to repel the besieging Romans. (Obelix can be seen as the reincarnation of the Breton Sun God and legendary original inhabitant of the peninsula, Gargantua. Whilst he was wandering through Brittany immense blocks of stone stuck, it is said, to the soles of Gargantua's shoes. He scraped them off and left them lying on the ground – the present-day standing stones.)

Inevitably the comic quality of the French original is sometimes lost in translation. But that does nothing to diminish the popularity of this frivolous epic packed with hilarious action. Time and again it brings us face to face with the absurdities in our habits, values and ideals.

✕ Food and drink

French provincial cooking, it turns out, is not at all *la grande cuisine*. Rather, the culinary arts of Brittany are born of traditional methods of preparing food, together with what is most distinctive about the local economy, and not least Brittany's situation almost entirely encircled by the sea. Breton recipes may lack refinement but they are substantial, nourishing and wholesome.

Anyone who likes fish and shellfish will find the cuisine particularly to his taste. Along the whole length of the coast, restaurants specialising in seafood abound: lobster, spiny lobster, crab, spider crab, oysters, mussels and scallops are served on a tangy seaweed garnished with ice. Breton *cotriade* – as much a stew as a soup – is made from a diverse assortment of fish such as dorado, perch, mackerel, bass, skate and turbot, together with shellfish, onions, carrots, potatoes, garlic, Calvados and white Muscadet wine. Lobster is boiled and served with mayonnaise or a piquant sauce, or it can be grilled. Alternatively, in a *pot-au-feu de homard Breton* it is cooked with other shellfish (oysters and mussels for example) in a broth, flavoured with leeks and onions, and enriched with Calvados and white wine; at the very last minute it is thickened with fresh cream. The famous Breton oysters (see pages 36–37) are eaten raw with a few drops of lemon juice.

As well as the seafood of the coastal region there are also freshwater fish to be found inland. Salmon frequent the Rivers Elorn and Aulne, and trout thrive in many places. Eels are caught in the moorland areas of the Brière, where they are eaten roasted over a peat fire.

Crêpes and galettes – a feast of pancakes

Crêperies are to be seen everywhere in the villages and towns. A thin batter prepared from flour, eggs, milk, water, sugar and vanilla is deftly spread over a hot circular iron griddle and fried. The finished pancakes are served either sprinkled with sugar or filled with jam, chocolate or apple purée before being folded into triangles or squares. Then there are the many varieties of *galette*, generously proportioned and ever-tempting; these are prepared in exactly the same way as crêpes but filled with eggs, fish or meat.

Alternatives to fish

The Bretons have a real taste for pork. *Kig-Ha-Farz* is a mixture of pork, beef, vegetables and boiled buckwheat. But if you really fancy something different you can sample wild duck or goose, rabbit, partridge, wild boar or moorland lamb. Lamb cutlets *prés salés* are a speciality of the coast around Mont-St-Michel – the meat from lambs grazed on the salt pastures is especially tasty. *Gigot aux haricots à la bretonne* is mutton served with green beans. These dishes are always accompanied by delicious fresh vegetables, the early Brittany vegetables being particularly good.

Cider, the traditional Breton low-alcohol apple drink, blends extremely well with all the local dishes. But Brittany has hardly any wine to call its own, the only native wine being the *Muscadet de Sèvre et Maine* from the area around Nantes (see page 43). However, wines from all over France are of course available.

Popular desserts include *far*, a kind of sweet batter-pudding often with dried fruit, *gâteau breton*, a rich Madeira cake, and *Kouing Ammann*, a crisp yeast cake. There are also many varieties of cheese to try, as there are throughout France.

Breton crêpes

Ingredients for 12 crêpes: ⅛ litre milk, 2 eggs, 1 egg yolk, 1 heaped tsp. caster sugar, the grated rind of ¼ lemon (one which has not been sprayed with chemicals), a pinch of salt, 75 g flour, 1 tbsp. brandy, 2 tbsp. melted butter, 2 tbsp. butter.

Method: Beat together the milk, eggs, egg yolk, sugar and salt. Sieve the flour on to the mixture, stirring in well. Mix in the brandy, lemon rind and melted butter, then leave for at least 30 minutes. Heat up an empty frying pan and grease lightly with butter. Pour in a portion of batter, letting it flow from the edge of the pan towards the centre. Cook the paper-thin *crêpes* on both sides. Fry the rest of the crêpes in the same way – keep them warm until ready to serve by piling them between two flat plates in an oven heated to 120°F/50°C (Gas mark 1).

Variation: For mushroom galettes leave out the sugar. Fill the prepared crêpes with 75 g sliced breakfast bacon (crisply fried), 250 g button mushrooms (sliced and sweated), 2 onions (chopped and sweated), 1 sprig of chervil or parsley, salt, black pepper and 3 tbsp. fresh cream.

Bon appétit!

Douarnenez harbour

The Breton way of life

In Armor, the coastal periphery of Brittany and region of highest population density (see pages 4–5), every Breton's livelihood is in some way connected with the sea, whether through shipping, fishing, ship-building and other marine trades or tourism. These are also the sectors in which Brittany's economic development is most advanced.

In fishing Brittany heads the French league with 44.6% of the total annual catch, its 2,234 boats representing 22% of the French fishing fleet. Shellfish and crustaceans also form an important part of the coastal fishing industry. Around fishing there has grown up a thriving secondary industry in food preservation which, out of the fishing season, switches to canning vegetables. Over-fishing of the coastal waters now means greater distances to be covered and higher fuel costs. Keen competition from the Japanese, Soviets and Americans with their floating fish factories makes the modernisation of vessels and processing techniques a matter of urgency if Brittany's fishing industry is to keep pace with the market.

Modern agriculture versus the hedged field

Argoat, the Breton name for the 'land of woods' (see pages 5–6), refers to the once extensively forested interior of the peninsula, long since forced to yield to the plough. The Breton *bocage*, a landscape in which hedges of shrubs and bushes divide the land, acting also as wind-breaks, is everywhere to be seen. Because these hedges stand in the way of modern technology-orientated land use, however, more and more of them are being cut down, and an increasing number of farms in what used to be a very varied landscape are being transformed into highly mechanised specialist enterprises. On 6% of France's agricultural land the Bretons today produce 3% of the nation's vegetables and 22% of its livestock. The ground is mainly used for cereals, root crops, fodder, vegetables and permanent pasture-land; Breton pig-, poultry- and dairy-farming have worked their way to the forefront of French animal husbandry. The food industry (fish-, vegetable- and meat-preserving) plays an extremely important role here too, the numbers employed being second only to those engaged in agriculture itself.

Jobs in industry and tourism

Not too long ago there was little industry in the peninsula except in the area around Nantes. When the French government adopted a policy of economic decentralisation however, to counter the growing problem of rural depopulation, Brittany was one of the regions to benefit, experiencing something of an economic surge. An improved infrastructure being an absolute necessity, Brittany was linked to the rest of France by new four-lane highways. 50,000 new jobs were created, many in branches of the Michelin tyre company, in Citroën cars, and in the electrical, food, construction and chemical industries.

Brittany today is also the second most important tourist region in France with about 3 million visitors a year. The largest number, of course, come from France itself, followed by the British, Irish, Germans and Belgians. In addition to the older-established resorts such as Dinard, St-Malo and La Baule, new centres of tourism have burgeoned. La Baule, Carnac, Quiberon, Tréboul, Roscoff, Perros-Guirec and St-Malo, all popular seaside holiday places, have also built up reputations as health spas (for thalassotherapy in particular, a treatment based on the sea air, seawater and salt). Inland, increasing efforts have been made over a number of years to boost the number of hotels offering a range of attractive holiday options. Unfortunately from an employment point of view, jobs in the tourist sector are only seasonal.

Bu hez hir c'hoaz d'ar yez koz!

'Long may the old language survive!' is the expression of a wish which the Breton people have had to fight hard to realise. A distinct Breton language had evolved here long before Brittany became a part of France. Called *brezoneg* it belongs to the Celtic family of languages, more specifically to a British branch which also includes Cornish and Cymric and which developed in parallel with the Irish and Scottish Gaelic tongues. It was brought from Britain in the 5th and 6th c. by Celts who, fleeing from the Angles and Saxons, settled in the peninsula. Together with Christianity it spread over the greater part of Brittany, local dialects subsequently being formed.

In the 14th and 15th c. the clergy and nobility considered it refined to converse in French, and the clergy in particular took care to prevent the ordinary people from learning the language of the upper classes, lest they should get ideas above their station.

Breton bocage

In the 19th c. Breton became a written language, and a Breton dictionary and grammar were compiled. At the same time however minority languages were beginning to be suppressed. Schoolchildren caught speaking Breton could expect to be the subject of scorn; not until 1951 was the ban lifted by the State. In 1977, following an initiative by the Bretons themselves, the language was once again permitted to be taught in private preparatory schools. Since then other schools have introduced Breton as an optional subject. The universities of Rennes and Brest now have Breton departments.

Crab-fisherman

Today over a million people are Breton-speaking. They are to be found especially in Finistère though the language is also spoken in parts of Côtes-du-Nord and Morbihan. In inland areas it is even still possible to meet elderly Bretons who cannot speak a word of French. And they are less than enthusiastic apparently about the new trend towards reviving the old language, claiming that the Breton to be heard on television and radio is not their mother tongue at all but a kind of pseudo-Breton, inauthentically pronounced.

Hints for your holiday

In many ways Brittany, the granite peninsula in north-west France, has been able to preserve its distinctive character despite a thoroughgoing process of modernisation. It continues to bear the imprint of a culture rooted deeply in primitive times.

This Celtic land girt by the Atlantic is sometimes described as wild and bleak. But with what truth? Surely the mimosa, the camellias and the fig-trees are the products rather of a gentleness, a mildness? Indeed the overpowering attraction of the peninsula lies precisely in the great charm of its chequered landscape, a landscape of so many different faces.

More than anyone it is French holidaymakers from the big conurbations who return to Brittany year after year. For the floodtide of tourists setting out from elsewhere, however, Brittany still does not figure as a major holiday destination. There are several reasons. For one thing the language is seen as something of a barrier. For another, with the exception of one or two places there is undoubtedly a shortage of hotel rooms and general provision for mass tourism (though there are plenty of *gîtes*, holiday cottages for rent). Finally, despite its mild climate under the benevolent influence of the Gulf Stream, the region offers no guarantee of sunshine and a tanned skin. The weather is typically capricious, with variable winds and rarely two days the same. Although Brittany is an ideal place to visit at any time of year, it is perhaps best to avoid the French holiday season in July and August – unless, that is, you are looking particularly for a beach holiday and also want to join in the traditional folk events, pilgrimages and harvest festivals.

Brittany's remarkable megalithic monuments and its ecclesiastical art of the Breton Renaissance – art which conveys so movingly a sense of the piety of the people – add further to the unique appeal of this land of myths and legends. And when you tire of studying the calvaries in Brittany's parish closes, innumerable seafood restaurants along the coast beckon with their culinary delights.

St-Malo

Where to go and what to see
Ille-et-Vilaine: Breton border strongholds

The department of Ille-et-Vilaine covers 6,932 sq km and has a population of 750,000. It takes its name from the Rivers Ille and Vilaine which converge at Rennes. This part of Brittany, with its great beaches and bays along the enchanting Côte d'Emeraude (Emerald Coast), its richly contrasting forests and moorland, and its mighty fortresses, was for a long time the Breton border country.

Rennes Pop. 205,000

Rennes lies at the centre of a fertile agricultural basin. The city has experienced rapid growth during one of the most turbulent periods of economic development in the region's history. On the outskirts modern multi-storey buildings have sprung up, while around the old historic nucleus on the north bank of the Vilaine imposing new residential districts have appeared amidst a profusion of parks – all vivid testimony to the pace of change. Rennes's favourable position as the meeting point of road, rail and air transport networks encouraged industry to relocate here. The result has been a significant expansion of the local economy, the benefits of which have

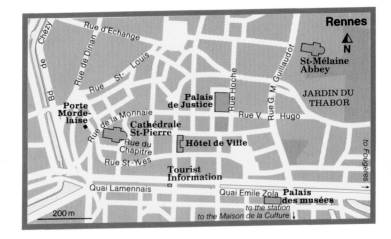

been felt in the surrounding countryside as well.

Diocesan centre, seat of the Breton parliament, administrative and financial hub of the region, in the 18th c. Rennes also acquired a university. Today it has two, which together with various colleges specialising in agriculture, electronics, public health, chemistry and administration are attended by about 27,000 students. This tradition of learning has also fostered the growth of a number of very active research establishments such as the Centre Commun d'Etudes de Télévision et de Télécommunication, as well as medical schools (including surgery) and an advanced electronics industry. Motor vehicles have been manufactured in Rennes since the sixties when the Citroën car factory became a show-piece for the policy of economic decentralisation. There are firms representing the food-processing industry, arms manufacture and road-building, in addition to a number of well-known printing and publishing houses. Being among France's premier regional newspapers the *Ober-*

thur and *Ouest-France* deserve special mention. The annual Rennes *International Trade Fair* and *Great Market* are symbols of the city's commercial vitality.

 From Celtic times to the 18th century

In Gallic times Rennes – then called *Condate* – was already the chief settlement of a Celtic tribe called the Redones. During the Middle Ages it was one of the mightiest fortress towns of the old French province of Marche. It became part of Brittany in 846 when Nominoë, having defeated Charles the Bald, was recognised by the French King as the first Breton ruler. After closer ties with France were once again restored in 1491 through the marriage of the Duchess Anne to Charles VIII, the city gained considerably in importance. In 1561 the Breton parliament was set up there, its main task being to preserve Breton autonomy in the face of increased centralisation of power in Paris. In 1720 large parts of Rennes with its lovely old houses were destroyed in a devastating fire. Rebuilt by the architect and town planner Jacques-Jules Gabriel, the city was laid out in classical style with wide streets running at right angles to one another. The fine town houses lining the squares in which the Hôtel de Ville and Palais de Justice stand are elegant and unadorned.

A walk through Old Rennes

A number of 14th and 15th c. houses in Le Vieux Rennes (Old Town) escaped the fire. One such, in the *Rue St-Guil-laume*, was the home of the great French military commander Bertrand du Guesclin who, in 1356, liberated Rennes from the besieging troops of Count Jean de Montfort. Today in this unusual half-timbered building with its projecting upper storeys a celebrated restaurant, *Ti Koz*, indulges its gourmet customers. There are a number of other old houses worth seeing in the nearby *Rue du Chapitre* (nos. 8 and 22, and the Hôtel de Blossac).

Palais de Justice: The beautiful *Place du Palais* is bordered by 17th and 18th c. houses as well as by the lawcourts. Formerly the parliament building the Palais de Justice, in Tuscan Renaissance style, was erected between 1618 and 1655, although the decoration of the interior was not completed until 1720. The grandeur of the building is revealed both in the classical façade and in the magnificent décor of the former parliament chamber, the *Grande Chambre*, with its gilded panelling, painted coffered ceilings and modern Gobelin tapestries depicting scenes from Breton history. The *Première Chambre*, which was also a parliamentary chamber, is less ornate but has instead superb wood panelling covered with paintings.

The Hôtel de Ville (town hall) in the Place de la Mairie was built between 1734 and 1743 by Jacques Gabriel in Louis Quinze style. It is particularly worth going in to see the grand staircase and hall, and the Hall of Remembrance dedicated to the dead of the First World War. Opposite the town hall stands the city's 19th c. *theatre*.

Cathédrale St-Pierre: Three different cathedrals have stood on this site since the 6th c., the present one having been completed in the 19th c. Of special interest is the 16th c. carved and gilded Flemish altarpiece. Facing the cathedral a road leads off the Rue de la Monnaie to the ruined *Porte Mordelaise*, a remnant of the city walls. In days gone by the dukes of Brittany passed through this gate to be crowned in the cathedral.

Museums: The *Palais des Musées,* a former university building on the Quai Emile Zola, houses the local history museum and the museum of fine art. Every aspect of Breton history and culture is covered in the *Musée de Bretagne*, including the megalithic and Gallo-Roman periods, the Middle Ages and the Ancien Régime. The *Musée des Beaux-Arts* possesses an excellent collection of paintings from the 14th c. to the present day. Some 4 km outside Rennes in the direction of Fougères (take the N12, Rue de Fougères) is the *Musée d'Automobiles* with a collection of vintage cars, motorcycles, bicycles and horse-drawn vehicles.

Parks: The one-time garden of the abbey of *St-Mélaine* (built in the 11th c., enlarged in the 14th and 17th c.) has been extended to create a 10-hectare public park, the *Jardin du Thabor*. Both it and the more intimate *Oberthur Park* are wonderfully inviting places to pause for a while and relax, as also are the tow-paths along the Rivers Ille and Vilaine.

 Ti Koz, 3 Rue la Chalotais: in Du Guesclin's half-timbered house (16th c. in its present form) complete with antique furnishings; *Au bon vieux temps*, Rue du Chapitre: comfortable crêperie; *La Chope*, Rue la Chalotais; *Le Corsaire*, 52 Rue d'Antrain; *Auberge St-Martin*, 230 Rue de St-Malo: fish specialities.

 Les Tombées de la nuit: street concerts, etc., during the annual 'Création Bretagne' festival held in Rennes in the second week of July.

Ex Around Rennes

From Rennes excursions can be made into the Vilaine valley, with its picturesque gorges, and to the Forêt de Rennes (Forest of Rennes) 11 km northeast of the city. Away to the west stretches the Paimpont forest and the countryside around Montfort, a landscape of narrow valleys, numerous ponds and abundantly wooded uplands. *Paimpont* forest, the fabled Brocéliande, once covered a large part of Brittany. It was here, so legend has it, that the wizard Merlin and fairy Vivien lived and loved. North-west of Rennes the 12th c. *Montauban* castle can be visited; it is situated on the edge of a stretch of forest bearing the same name. Some 13 km further north are two more castles, *Caradeuc*, a classical château close to Bécherel and, 1 km north of Les Iffs, *Montmuran* (12th–18th c.).

Redon Pop. 10,250

Standing at the crossing of two waterways – the River Vilaine and the Nantes–Brest Canal – Redon has developed into an important river port. Sub-prefecture of the department of Ille-et-Vilaine it is also an agricultural centre (with a famous chestnut-market) and has some industry. Rising high above the transept crossing of Redon's church of *St-Sauveur* is a lovely Romanesque tower with three arcaded storeys and small corner towers. Inside the church some Romanesque elements survive and some fragments of frescos can still be seen. The Gothic belfry became separated from the main building after a fire in 1780.

 Musicomania festival in July.

Ex La Roche-aux-Fées

18 km north of Redon and some 2 km off to the left from the D177 to Rennes lies the little town of *St-Just*, around which is an area rich in megaliths. The most magnificent megalithic monument of all in the east of Armorica, however, is La Roche-aux-Fées (The Fairies' Stone), about 27 km north of Châteaubriant. This massive dolmen consisting of thirty-three upright stones bearing the weight of eight large roof-slabs is entered through an antechamber. Its age has been estimated as 4,500 years.

A special tip

The canals of Brittany nowadays provide a novel way of seeing the country. You can either join one of the organised tours on these delightful waterways or hire a boat yourself. They can be hired at Redon from Location de Pénichettes, 12 Quai Jean-Bart.

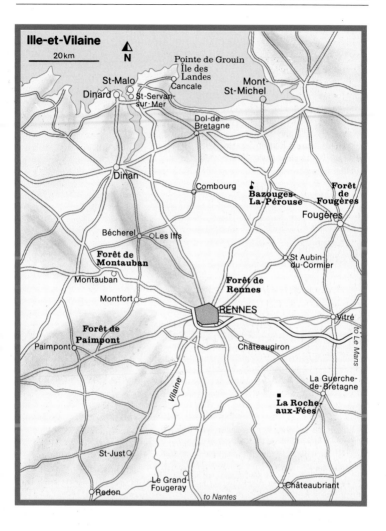

Frontier strongholds on Brittany's eastern border

Along the eastern border of Brittany lie a string of mighty fortresses and castles – Fougères, St-Aubin-du-Cormier, Vitré, Châteaugiron, La Guerche-de-Bretagne, Blain, Le Grand-Fougeray and Châteaubriant – frontier strongholds whose military effectiveness was conceded by Louis XI himself. Vitré and Fougères are chosen here as examples of these important fortress towns.

Vitré Pop. 12,000

The castle, which dates back to the 11th c. and was extended in the 14th c. and again in the 15th c., stands enthroned on the outermost point of a rocky spur above the River Vilaine. With its high walls (along which you can walk) and its towers majestically crowned by battlements, pinnacles and pointed roofs, the building is a masterpiece of Breton military architecture. Entrance to the inner precinct is gained via a drawbridge. The Montafilant Tower provides a glorious view over the town, while elsewhere in the castle is housed a museum of history and art.

In the town of Vitré itself well-preserved alleyways of old houses complete the air of medieval charm. In the square at the end of the Rue Notre-Dame the 15th and 16th c. church of *Notre-Dame* is worth visiting on account of a triptych to be found in the sacristy. The enamelled panels were made in Limoges.

 Le petit Billot, 5 Place du Général Leclerc.

Fougères Pop. 30,000

This magnificent stronghold with its thirteen towers was provided with additional protection by the diverting of the River Nançon so as to complete an encircling loop. Built in the 11th c. and extended in the centuries that followed, Fougères was the mightiest of all the medieval Breton fortresses.

For a rewarding tour of the ramparts on foot proceed in a clockwise direction along the Rue Le-Bouteiller. Easily recognised as you come to them are: the

Vitré

The fortress, Fougères

Fougères

square 13th c. sundial tower known as the *Tour de Cadran*; the *Tour Raoul* and *Tour Surienne* (horseshoe-shaped towers from the final phase of building in the 15th c.); and the circular *Mélusine* and *Gobelin Towers*, built in the 13th and 14th c. Behind the Gobelin Tower there was at one time a keep, but this was razed in 1166 by the English King Henry II following his capture of the town. Arriving at the Boulevard de Rennes you should pause to admire at a distance the towers of the north rampart – the 14th c. *Guibé Turret* (in the centre of this section of wall) and the *Coigny Tower*, the second and third storeys of which were converted into a chapel in the 17th c.

The inner precincts of the fortress can also be visited though sadly most of the buildings are now in ruins. Only the towers and walls still survive. A small museum of Breton furniture is housed in the Raoul Tower, while in the Surienne Tower there is a museum tracing the history of shoemaking. The reputation Fougères enjoys for the manufacture of ladies' shoes was established in the last century.

 St-Sulpice

This 15th to 18th c. church with graceful central spire is definitely worth a visit simply on account of its granite retable. In addition however the south door is framed by an attractive border decorated in a leaf motif, while a niche in the adjacent wall is graced by the sculpted figure of a naked maiden combing her hair. This is the Celtic fairy Mélusine, her presence a reminder that when the valley of the Nançon was still a marshy wetland its inhabitants used to worship water goddesses.

 Les Voyageurs, 10 Place Gambetta: good food.

Around Fougères

North of Fougères is the Fougères State Forest within which there are a number of megalithic monuments. On a bluff about 25 km north-west of Fougères lies the small town of Antrain-sur-Couesnon, 1 km south of which is a fine 16th c. château, *Bonne-Fontaine*, set in a lovely park. From there the D796 leads to another interesting castle (10th–16th c.) at Bazouges-la-Pérouse. Although privately owned its delightful gardens are open to the public. The next stop is Combourg.

Combourg Pop. 5,000

In this idyllic little town dominated by its great medieval château the French Romantic writer François-René de Chateaubriand (1768–1848) spent part of his youth. The forbidding castle (built in the 11th c. and enlarged in the 14th and 15th c.) was acquired by Chateaubriand's father in 1761, and the writer describes his early life here in his *Mémoires d'Outre-Tombe* (Memoirs from beyond the grave). Some of the rooms have been turned into a museum dedicated to him.

 Du Château, 1 Place Chateaubriand.

Head north from Combourg. A short distance before Dol-de-Bretagne, on the right-hand side and only a few hundred metres from the road, towers the 9.3-m-high *Champ-Dolent* menhir (the name means 'place of suffering').

Dol-de-Bretagne Pop. 5,000

It was here at Dol-de-Bretagne around 848 that Nominoë was crowned the first duke of Brittany. The town is the centre of a bishopric and has a well-preserved Old Quarter. The early importance of the diocese is reflected in the cathedral, *St-Samson*, an impressive Gothic building of unusual proportions. The porch on the south side and the beautiful choir stalls (14th c.) are exceptional.

In 709 the whole area suffered catastrophic inundation by the sea, as a result of which the coastline was moved inland as far as Dol. In the 12th c. this tract of land, known today as the *Marais de Dol* (Dol Marsh), was successfully reclaimed and became fertile ploughland.

 Grand Hôtel de la Gare, 21 Av Aristide Briand: seafood, salmon, lamb.

St-Malo Pop. 48,000

This town of granite seems almost to be one with the rocks on which it has grown, rocks which once formed an island washed by the surf and which only later became linked to the mainland by a narrow strip of land. This is the old, impregnable St-Malo, refuge of privateers on the Emerald Coast. Squeezed within the high walls against which the tide hurls itself twice a day are the streets and buildings of the Ville Close or 'cité intra-muros', as the historic nucleus of the town is known.

 The history of this coastal town

The earliest settlement here, named *Aleth*, dated from Gallo-Roman times. In the 6th c. its inhabitants were converted to Christianity by Malo (also called Maclou), a monk and recluse who later became their bishop.

During the 9th c. Aleth was under constant threat of attack by the Normans so in search of greater security the people resettled themselves on a neighbouring island where Malo had been buried. The seat of the bishop was eventually transferred there in the 12th

c. and the little town acquired the name 'St-Malo'.

In peacetime it sent its ships all over the world, establishing fruitful links with, for example, the Hanseatic League in north Germany. In times of war its sailors became privateers, boldly and defiantly attacking the English and the Dutch. Its famous citizens include the astronomer-mathematician and philosopher Maupertuis, and the writer-statesman Chateaubriand (see page 33). Right up till the 20th c. St-Malo proved impregnable against attack by sea. With the Allied landings in 1944 however the great port was largely destroyed, only to be restored again after the War, faithfully rebuilt in the appropriate historical styles. In 1967 the municipalities of St-Servan, Paramé and St-Malo joined together to form a single administrative district in order to promote the development of the port and also tourism.

 A walk round the town

There is a delightful walk along the top of the ramparts, the round trip taking about 1½ hours. The main steps on to the ramparts are at the *Porte St-Vincent* which is a short distance south of the castle's great keep. The views are superb: out over the yacht harbour and the commercial port, the sea and the sandy beach; down into the depths of the streets enclosed within the walls; across to the island of *Grand Bé* where Chateaubriand's tomb lies among the rocks; and to the *Fort National*, a stronghold on a rocky islet, built by Vauban and used for a time as a prison. At low tide the fort can be reached on foot. The 15th c. *castle*, another imposing fortress with four towers, protected the Ville Close from assault by land. As well as being the town hall and library the castle houses the St-Malo *museum* (Musée de la Ville) in the great keep or

St-Malo – architecture and atmosphere

Sunbathing at St-Malo

donjon. There is a *waxworks* in the Quic-en-Groigne Tower. In the nearby Place Vauban is an *aquarium*, and diagonally opposite it an *exotarium*. The alleyways of the Ville Close are full of atmosphere with their souvenir shops, restaurants, bars and street cafés. Over Malo's burial place there now stands the cathedral of *St-Vincent*, a mainly Gothic building although the façade dates from the 18th c. The chancel (13th c.) has beautiful stained-glass windows.

St-Servan-sur-Mer just to the south is now a district of St-Malo. It possesses lovely sandy beaches and three harbours. Along what is known as the *Corniche d'Aleth* which runs round St-Servan's rocky promontory, a walk high above the shore affords fine views of St-Malo, the port, the Rance estuary and the sea. On the southern side of the promontory the *Tour Solidor* built in 1382 still stands guard over the Rance. Inside the tower is the interesting Musée International du Long Cours Cap-Hornier, a sailing-ship museum devoted to 'Cape Horners'.

The seaside resort of St-Malo, bulging with hotels, is actually to be found at *Paramé* a little way to the north where an attractive promenade

several kilometres long is lined with villas surviving from the resort's earliest days. Paramé merges without a break into *Rothéneuf*, distinguished by its almost village atmosphere. Here there are beaches backed by dunes and cliffs.

 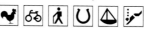

 Fish specialities: *Casino*, 2 Chaussée du Sillon; *Le Chalut*, 8 Rue Corne de Cerf; *La Métairie de Beauregard*; *Le Servannais*, 4 Rue Amiral Magon.

Cabaret, theatre, casino.

H Thalassotherapy.

Hydrofoil and ferry connections to Guernsey, Jersey and Sark. Ferry to Portsmouth. Boats run to the Île de Cézembre near St-Malo and also to Dinard on the west bank of the Rance estuary (every 10 minutes).

Ex **Excursions on the Emerald Coast**

From Rothéneuf take the exceptionally pleasant coastal road (D201) to the *Pointe du Grouin* (hotel, restaurant), a wild, rocky tongue of land, ruggedly beautiful, with a distant view of Mont-St-Michel. Offshore to the east stretches the long *Île des Landes*, now a nature reserve.

Cancale: A short distance further along the coast (4 km south of the Pointe) the little town of Cancale (population about 5,000), famous for its oysters, lies on the shallow *Baie du Mont-St-Michel*. Oysters have been cultivated at Cancale from Antiquity. The best time to see it is at low water when the oyster-beds are exposed and the oystermen's work can begin.

Lining the quayside are innumerable restaurants and cafés where you can sample the local oysters and other seafood specialities. *Le Continental*, 4 Quai A. D. Thomas: seafood platter, grilled lobster *Michel St Cast*, *œufs océaniques* ('ocean eggs'); *Le Phare*: scallops, Cancale sole.

Dinan Pop. 16,400

The drive from St-Malo to this small medieval town in the department of Côtes-du-Nord makes a charming outing (Dinan is also easily reached from

Dinan Castle

Restaurant in Dinan

St-Malo by boat). The town is enchantingly sited on a 70-m-high plateau, which slopes steeply down into the valley of the Rance. Waiting to be discovered in the historic town centre – sheltering behind its ramparts – are many old houses and quaint little shops, reminiscent of another era. Art dealers, glass-blowers and wood-carvers have all established themselves here, adding to the town's atmosphere.

St-Sauveur is a mainly Late Gothic basilica church with a Romanesque porch. The nave is marked by a distinct lack of symmetry. From the top of the town's magnificent 60-m-high *Tour de l'Horloge* (15th c.) there is a marvellous panoramic view to be enjoyed.

The 14th–15th c. *castle* occupies a commanding position high above the ramparts. Inside is a museum devoted to the history of Dinan. The beautiful Promenade des Grands Fossés and equally beautiful Promenade des Petits Fossés, both of which skirt the ramparts, should not be missed.

Chez la Mère Pourcel, 3 Place des Merciers: beautiful half-timbered house (15th c.), comfortable and old-fashioned; *Hôtel de France*, 7 Place du 11 novembre; *Merveilles des Mers*, on the Rance embankment: pretty view.

Harvesting a yield from the sea

Farmers of the tidal shore

Oysters, an iodine- and vitamin-rich delicacy, provide a dish of wonderfully refreshing simplicity when eaten straight from the oyster-beds and sprinkled with nothing more than lemon juice. Cancale alone produces about a quarter of France's oysters, but round the Breton coast there are other well-known oyster-growing areas – between Concarneau and Lorient, in the bay of

Breton oysters

St-Brieuc, in the Golfe du Morbihan and in the Avens des Finistère. The men who cultivate the oysters clatter back and forth in their amphibious vehicles to the rhythm of the tides, tending the neat rows of beds night and day. When the cold winter of 1963 killed off the whole breeding stock of flat oysters, the growers were forced to switch to the hollow variety. Cold and parasites are the oyster-breeders' chief enemies. The oysters are kept in perforated plastic trays secured to metal tables. At the beginning of the summer the adult oysters produce their larvae, which settle on a kind of larva-trap – a device which looks like a concave brick. After three months when the larvae have grown to 3 cm they are scraped off and placed in the flat oyster-beds to continue growing for several years. Until maturity (which they reach in about three years) they are kept at a warmish temperature in plankton-rich water – from where they go straight to the gourmet's plate.

Energy from ebb and flood – the St-Malo tidal power station

Tidal water flooding from the Atlantic Ocean up the English Channel is checked by the Channel Islands and the Cotentin Peninsula. The resulting 'pile-up' of water produces a tidal range of 13.5 m in the Baie de St-Malo, the highest anywhere in the world. Visitors to Brittany are always fascinated by the ebb and flow of the tides, and nowhere more so than at the *usine marémotrice* (tidal power station) at the mouth of the Rance. Between Dinard and St-Malo a 700-m-long barrage complete with lock closes off the Rance estuary from the sea. The generator-house with its twenty-four turbine generators is built into the dam and is open to visitors. Also to be seen are the great sluices with their six gigantic gates through which the Rance basin empties and fills. On the flood 18,000 cu. m of water streams into the basin every second. By adjusting the turbine blades it is possible to make use of both the flood tide and the receding ebb. 545 million kWh are produced by 184 million cu. m of water. A power station like this however is incapable of producing energy on a continuous basis since its turbines stand idle during the period of slack water.

Dinard beach

Dinard Pop. 10,000

Dinard, the best-known resort on the north coast of Brittany, extends along the west bank of the Rance opposite St-Malo. It has been popular with British and American visitors for over a century, a fact which has influenced the architecture of the town. It is a smart place, somewhat old-fashioned, with excellent beaches and good bathing (including a seawater swimming pool). From the *Pointe du Moulinet* there are splendid views of the Rance estuary, St-Malo and the sea, while the walk along the 'Moonlight Promenade' is particularly enchanting. Anyone seeking a typical Breton Old Town ambience, however, will search Dinard in vain.

 Le Trézen, 3 Bd Féart: seafaring atmosphere; *Des Bains*, 38 Av George V: fish specialities; *Du Roy*, 8 Bd Féart: crêperie.

 The crossing to St-Malo takes less than 10 minutes.

  18-hole course.

 Aquarium and maritime museum.

 St-Lunaire (pop. 1,500) to the west of Dinard, an elegant seaside resort with sandy beaches; *St-Briac-sur-Mer* (pop. 1,600), somewhat quieter with a fishing and yacht harbour and fine beaches. There is a splendid view over to Cap Fréhel from *La Garde Guérin*, a headland midway between the two.

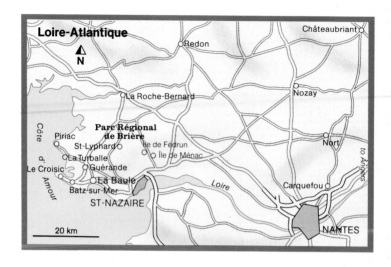

Loire-Atlantique: salt-pans, marshland and fashionable resorts

In 1962 when France was split up into a number of economic and administrative regions the department of Loire-Atlantique was lost to Brittany. This was despite the fact that Nantes, chief town of the department, had for a long time been the Breton capital. In view of its historic connections with Brittany the northern part of Loire-Atlantique has been included in this guide. It is primarily its coast that makes Loire-Atlantique a popular holiday destination – a strip of shoreline about 130 km long encompassing the Côte d'Amour, the Côte de Jade and the Vendée Coast, with small secluded bays alternating with long sandy beaches backed by dunes and pine woods. In addition the department possesses an attractive hinterland, enriched by its mix of cultural elements drawn from Brittany, Anjou and the Vendée.

Nantes Pop. 430,000

Nantes – birthplace of the author Jules Verne (1828–1905) – took its name from the first people to settle in the area, a Celtic tribe called the Namnetes. In Roman times it was already an established trading centre. Today Nantes, once the seat of the dukes of Brittany, is the chief town of Loire-Atlantique and 'capital' of the western Loire area. It sits astride the main traffic routes between Brittany and the Loire Valley. As well as being a major commercial port it is an industrial and cultural centre and a university city. It is also the hub of a number of thriving tourist areas.

The once traditional industries of the coastal region have today given way to new ventures, though food processing remains important, sustained by good-quality agricultural produce. Reorganisation of the shipbuilding industry has involved considerable support from the State. Some firms have turned to the

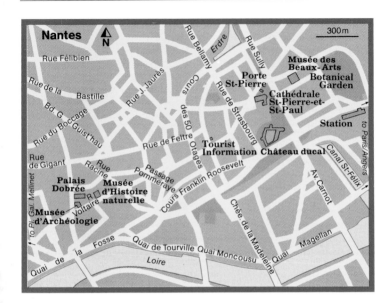

nuclear power industry, others to the oil industry or mechanical engineering. A successful international trade fair is held annually in the Palais de la Beaujoire. Every five years the Beaujoire also hosts the *Floralies Internationales*, which has given Nantes the title of 'Ville Fleurie' (City of Flowers). The *Centre de Communication de l'Ouest* (Western Centre for Communication) is the only one of its kind in France.

 Sightseeing

Lovely buildings like the old Breton ducal palace, the cathedral, the Graslin Theatre and the Passage Pommeraye bear striking witness to the richness of the city's past.

The Château Ducal and its museums:
The ducal palace at Nantes is an impressive moated stronghold. It was begun in 1466 by François II, Duke of Brittany (1435–88), and continued by his daughter Anne de Bretagne (1477–1514) after 1491 – the year of her marriage to Charles VIII, King of France. From the 17th c. to the end of the First World War the castle served as a barracks. In 1800 a whole wing was destroyed when the powder magazine in the Tour des Espagnols (Spaniards' Tower) exploded.

In 1915 the palace passed into the possession of the city and with the opening of the *Museum of Art and Crafts* took on a new role – documenting life in old Brittany. In the *Tour de Fer à cheval* (Horseshoe Tower) there is a collection of works by contemporary artists in textiles.

The *Salorges Museum* is devoted to the trading, colonial and industrial history of Nantes from the 18th c. and was founded by two Nantes canning-factory owners. Bequeathed to the city in 1954 it is now housed in the Harness Building where regimental horses were once bridled.

In the building known as Le Grand Gouvernement is a *Musée d'Art Populaire Régional* (Museum of Popular Art). The collection includes costumes and furniture from the 16th to the early 20th c.

Cathédrale St-Pierre-et-St-Paul: The cathedral was begun (on 4th c. foundations) in 1434 but completed only in 1893. Two austere towers flank the long Flamboyant-style nave. After a fire in 1972 large parts of the building had to be restored. The most impressive piece of ornamentation in the interior is unquestionably the tomb of Anne de Bretagne's parents, François II and Marguerite de Foix. This masterpiece by the Breton sculptor Michel Colombe is acknowledged to be one of the very finest examples of Renaissance art.

Standing close to the north side of the cathedral is the *Porte St-Pierre*, a 15th c. gateway built on the remains of the 3rd c. city wall. The Late Gothic *Psalette* on the cathedral's south side was formerly the chapter-house.

Museums, and yet more museums: Nantes is a city of museums. The *Musée des Beaux-Arts* (Museum of Fine Arts), 10 Rue Georges Clemenceau, has a collection of paintings from the 13th to the 20th c. (de la Tour, Ingres, Courbet). The *Musée Thomas Dobrée* (Palais Dobrée) in the Place Jean V was

Cathedral and Place Maréchal Foch, Nantes

founded in the 19th c. by a local ship-owner. As well as paintings and prints the collection includes Romanesque and Gothic works of art, among them a precious reliquary containing the heart of Anne de Bretagne.

On display in the *Musée d'Archéologie* (Regional Archaeological Museum) in the Rue Voltaire are fragments from long-vanished buildings both secular and religious.

Among other collections are the *Doll and Antique Toy Museum*, 39 Bd St-Aignau, the *Printing Museum*, 24 Quai de la Fosse, the *Musée d'Histoire Naturelle*, 12 Rue Voltaire (one of the best museums of its kind in France for zoology, palaeontology and mineralogy), the *Jules Verne Museum*, 3 Rue de l'Hermitage, and the *Postal Museum*, 10 Bd Pageot, which, in addition to housing a stamp collection, traces the development of the postal service. Finally there is the *Planetarium*, 8 Rue des Acadiens, where the night sky is shown projected on to a hemispherical dome.

Half-timbered houses and town mansions: On the Place de Change is the 15th c. half-timbered *Maison des Apothicaires*. Other half-timbered houses have been preserved in the Rue de l'Emery. The Place Général Mellinet is lined by splendid Charles X town mansions. On the far side of the Cours Franklin Roosevelt is the former *Île Feydeau*, originally encircled by a small arm of the Loire before it was filled in. The buildings of the Île provide some fine examples of 18th c. architecture and testify to the wealth of the shipowners of Nantes (mascarons, bas-reliefs, ornamental balconies).

Passage Pommeraye: On the way back to the old quarter of the city go via the Passage Pommeraye, a part of Nantes that seems somehow surreal. The arcade with its unusual glass dome, galleries, stucco-work, busts and statues seems to stand apart from everything else in time and space. It was built in 1843. Stairways lead up to shops on three floors. *La Cigale* (the Cicada restaurant) is a truly remarkable monument to the 19th c. With its huge mirrors, its ceilings adorned with pictures, its statues and its lamps, it used to be the meeting place of Belle Epoque high society.

Green spaces: The city's many parks and gardens are havens of peace and relaxation. The *Botanical Garden* opposite the railway station possesses a unique collection of 400 varieties of camellia. There are azaleas and rhododendrons in the *Parc de Procé*, and lovely paths along the Chézine. The *Parc de la Beaujoire* makes a speciality of its irises and heathers, while the *Grand Blotterau* boasts tropical hothouses. *Versailles Island* with its Japanese garden rounds off a list of delightful possibilities.

 Terrasse Décre, 20 Rue de la Marne.

A special tip
The gentle Erdre which flows into the Nantes–Brest Canal provides the perfect setting for a river trip. Enjoy a gastronomic pilgrimage at a pace set by the rhythm of the locks. Grands Bateaux de l'Erdre shipping company (River Palace), 24 Quai de Versailles.

Châteaubriant Pop. 14,000

Situated to the north of Nantes, Châteaubriant, along with the strongholds of Fougères, Vitré and Ancenis, once

Nantes–Brest Canal

formed the gateway to the Duchy of Brittany. Its mighty castle still towers above the River Chère though little of the original feudal fortress now remains. Construction of the castle was begun in the 11th c. by a nobleman called Briant who gave the castle and town his name.

Some considerable time later another count of Châteaubriant married one Françoise de Foix while she was still a child. She became the mistress of François I but when she was replaced at court by a rival was taken back to Châteaubriant by her jealous husband. She was imprisoned in a room in the castle where she is thought to have remained for the next ten years. It is possible that in the end she was murdered by the Count.

The castle consists of two distinct complexes: the medieval Vieux-Château dating back to the 11th c. and the Château-Neuf (1533–39) built during the Renaissance period.

In the north-westernmost part of the town, the district known as Béré, the road to Rennes is graced by the splendid red sandstone façade of the church of *St-Jean-de-Béré*. The chancel and transept are 11th c. and the nave 12th c. The fine bas-reliefs on the exterior are noteworthy, as are the altars within.

A special tip

To the south of Nantes and along the Loire Valley stretch 12,000 hectares of vineyards planted mainly with *Muscadet* (80%) but also with some *Gros Plant* (20%). These produce light, unassuming wines, with all the exuberance of the nearby ocean. Gros Plant is not quite up to the standard of Muscadet — refreshing but a little acid — going well however with shellfish and oysters. The Gros Plant vineyards lie to the west of Nantes in the Pays de Retz. The best Muscadet is produced in the area known as *Sèvre et Maine*, where the loose and stony soils found between the Rivers Sèvre and Maine give the wine its pleasant taste.

The Côte d'Amour

The 130-km-long shoreline of Loire-Atlantique is split in two by the Loire estuary as it opens out into the Atlantic. A bridge over the river at St-Nazaire — sheer length (3,356 m) makes it the most impressive bridge in Europe — links the coasts on either side, the *Côte de Jade* to the south, which takes its name from the colour of the ocean, and the *Côte d'Amour* (the Lovers' Coast) to the north. Only the latter is included here.

St-Nazaire Pop. 69,800

St-Nazaire has important shipyards and has experienced an economic upturn

La Baule

since the fashion for ever-larger ships has meant that deep-draught vessels can no longer reach Nantes. The harbour and the harbour promenade, the former submarine base, the shipyards and the Loire bridge (mentioned above) are all worth seeing.

 The seaside resort of *Pornichet* now joined to La Baule has splendid sandy beaches; the well-known *Hippodrome de la Côte d'Amour* (racecourse) is also situated here.

 Thalassotherapy.

La Baule Pop. 15,200

La Baule, the region's main seaside resort, is noted for its modernity and its 9-km-long sandy beach. It is one of those resorts which, with ballrooms, casinos, and ornate villas set among pines, evoke the Belle Epoque. Ultramodern luxury hotels as well as casinos and restaurants line the elegant 5-km-long promenade. La Baule is popular with people who enjoy activity holidays.

 Thalassotherapy.

 There is a beautiful walk along *La Grande Côte*, a lovely stretch of

the shore with sandy bays, and grottos which can be reached at low water.

 Harbour (for fishing boats and pleasure craft) in the channel separating La Baule from *Le Pouliguen* (pop. 4,300).

Batz-sur-Mer Pop. 2,300

With the 60-m-high belfry of St-Guénolé visible for miles around this little Breton town once kept watch between ocean and marsh. If you climb the steep narrow steps of the belfry you will be rewarded with a superb panorama over the wide expanse of countryside, with the salt marshes, the *marais salants*, to the north-east.

Loam and sparkling white salt lie in heaps around the salt-pans, the salt garnered from the marshes being brought for packaging in Batz. This area is under economic threat from its rivals in the Mediterranean where the evaporation process is much quicker. On feast days the traditional costumes of the salt-makers are much in evidence.

Smaller seaside resorts: Still on the Côte d'Amour *Le Croisic* boasts a fishing and yacht harbour, aquarium and naval museum as well as some fine old houses dating from the 15th and 17th c. The harbour at *La Turballe* is home to the largest fleet of sardine boats on the Atlantic coast. *Piriac*, another fishing village, has 17th c. half-timbered houses.

Guérande, situated on the northern side of the salt marshes in the centre of the Guérande peninsula, has retained its medieval atmosphere. Four gateways lead into the Old Town with its encircling ramparts, the latter further fortified by another six towers. The *Château St-Michel*, one of the four gatehouses, used to be the governor's residence and is now a small museum. The church of *St-Aubin*, begun in the 12th c., was not completed till the 16th c. North of the town the *Moulin du Diable* (Devil's Mill) stands near a dolmen on the right-hand side of the D774.

The Brière Regional Park

Go just a little way inland from any of the resorts on the Côte d'Amour and you enter the 7,000-hectare Brière nature reserve. The special charm of the area lies in the tranquillity of the marshland, its meres overgrown with reeds and rushes, its canals and channels, sometimes straight, sometimes winding, stretching to the horizon, and its villages (many of them islets with island names – Île de Fédrun, Île de Ménac), close-knit clusters of small, thatched-roofed, white-painted houses. Only a single road crosses this strange landscape, originally a sea gulf into which the Rivers Vilaine and Loire flowed. They deposited their sediments here and so the marshland evolved.

Since 1462 this whole area of swampland – the largest in France after the Camargue – has been ground held in common by all Briérons. In 1970 the regional nature reserve was created. The secrets of this unique habitat with its rich variety of plants and animals are best explored by boat (trips being arranged from several places). Grande Brière is revealed as a mosaic of waterways, small weirs, water-meadows and hummocks.

For centuries the surface peat was the marsh-dwellers' only form of fuel. Today many Briérons have been forced to leave the marshes because there is no longer a dependable living to be made in the traditional ways – from fishing, hunting, cutting peat and gathering reeds for thatching. They have set-

tled in places which offer the security of an assured income. Cattle-rearing is also in decline as a result, and the whole marshland area is beginning to clog with reeds. The canals are no longer regularly maintained and this is already having its effect on the flora and fauna.

Museums of local history and wildlife

Rosé–St-Malo-de-Guersac: Museum in the lock-keeper's house (history, economy and traditional occupations of the Brière), wildlife park (marsh birds in their natural setting), natural history (display of stuffed marshland animals, fish in aquaria).

Fédrun–St-Joachim: Briéron thatched farmhouse museum (stuffed birds, costumes).

St-Lyphard: Kerhinet Museum (typical Grande Brière house, drawings, paintings, tools), artisan's house (arts and crafts), several exhibitions; megalithic grave-mound at Dissignac.

House in the Brière

Vannes

Morbihan: dolmens and menhirs

The southern coast of Brittany between La Roche-Bernard (to the south-east) and Lorient (to the north-west) comprises the department of Morbihan — the name, Breton in origin, means 'little sea'. It is a region of great charm, a charm which stems from ancient villages and small market towns, old castles, parish closes, a multitude of megalithic cult and burial sites set in lonely heathland, spacious white sandy beaches, coasts with cliffs pierced by natural arches, a mild, temperate climate, and, last but not least, France's largest inland sea — the Golfe du Morbihan. Dotted with innumerable islands — the Île d'Arz and Île aux Moines are the biggest — the gulf is about 20 km across and linked to the open Atlantic by a channel about 1 km wide. One can well imagine what dangerous tidal currents are generated here. Many of the gulf's rocks appear only at low water.

Vannes Pop. 43,500

Vannes, administrative centre of Morbihan and one of seven bishoprics in Brittany, lies on the northern side of the Golfe du Morbihan. A number of small rivers converge here, widening south of the town to form the harbour and a passage to the sea (vessels are able to enter the harbour only at high water, however). This busy commercial town into which some modern industry has moved (Michelin tyres) has grown up around its cathedral. There are some well-preserved half-timbered houses. After uniting all of Brittany Nominoë, the commoner originally appointed Duke of Vannes by Louis the Pious in 826, ruled his new territory from Vannes, and following the Breton War of Succession Vannes temporarily became the ducal capital again.

The Old Town

The medieval ramparts and gateways survive, as does the old wash-house (all of these are floodlit at night). There are some especially pretty half-timbered houses in the Rue des Chanoines, the Rue St-Guenhaël and the Place Henri IV. The most famous however is the *Maison de Vannes* in the Rue Noë. *Château Gaillard* in the same street, the former seat of the Breton parliament, is now the Archaeological Museum, and contains a large number of finds from prehistoric times.

The cathedral of *St-Pierre* (13th–19th c.) is mainly Flamboyant in style, an exception being the round chapel, built in 1537 and modelled on Italian Renaissance designs. In the cathedral is the tomb of St Vincent Ferrer, a Spanish monk who died in Vannes in 1419. Also of interest are the tapestries and the cathedral treasures. Opposite the cathedral, on the first floor of La Cohue, the former covered market (12th and 14th c.), is the *Musée des Beaux-Arts*.

Vannes possesses one of the largest aquaria in Europe. It is situated by the pleasure-boat harbour.

 Le Roof, Presqu'île de Conleau: fish, Breton fare; *A l'Image Ste Anne,* 8 Place de la Libération: fish specialities.

Ex **Boat trips**

There are sailings across the Golfe du Morbihan calling at the Île d'Arz and Île aux Moines, and then the small towns of Port-Navalo and Locmariaquer, before continuing a little way up the River Auray. They are organised by *Les Vedettes Vertes du Golfe*, Parc du Golfe, Gare Maritime.

Vannes

The southern side of the gulf to Port-Navalo

From Vannes head for the Rhuys peninsula, an area blessed with a lovely climate and an abundance of Mediterranean plants such as fig-trees, camellias and myrtles. First landmark *en route* is *Kerlévenan*, a castle with classical façade.

Next stop should be at the 15-m-high *Tumiac* tumulus, a royal tomb, before you drive on to the westernmost point of the peninsula, *Port-Navalo*, from where there is a stupendous view of the entrance to the gulf. *St-Gildas-de-Rhuys* in the south-west of the peninsula came into being in the year 530, with the founding of a monastery there by St Gildas. The Romanesque chancel and transept have survived in the abbey church, but the remainder was largely rebuilt in the 16th and 17th c. The church treasures (reliquaries, ancient measures, etc.) are also particularly worth seeing.

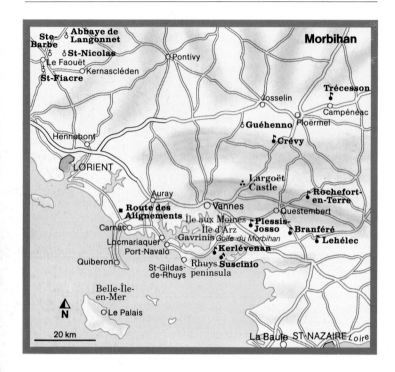

Tour of the ducal palaces

Suscinio: Returning from Rhuys, follow the D198 to the once mighty Suscinio Castle (13th c.), now an impressive and romantic ruin. This former summer residence of the dukes of Brittany makes a good starting point for a tour of the ducal palaces.

Plessis-Josso, a manor house built by Duke Jean III in 1330, and fortified and enlarged in the 15th and 16th c., stands on the right-hand side of the D183 between Surzur and Le Gorvello.

Rochefort-en-Terre: The D7 which passes through the little town of Questembert continues as the D777 to Rochefort-en-Terre. Here the surviving parts of the castle (14th–15th c.) – originally started by the lords of Rochefort and Rieux and still bearing their name – have been beautifully preserved. Paintings and many other works of art can be viewed in the interior.

Lehélec: Take the D774 south towards Péaule, turning left on to the D20. Lehélec Château is to the right about 8 kilometres further on. The 17th c. house is surrounded by 16th c. outbuildings, inside one of which is a small museum of antique furniture.

Branféré: Finally go back to Péaule and then via Le Guerno to Branféré Château a few kilometres further north-east. The attraction of the château is its zoo park where 2,000 animals including some rare ones inhabit a large area of parkland planted with exotic trees.

More castles to the north of Vannes

In the countryside to the north of Vannes are a number of castles which are well worth visiting.

Largoët: Take the N166 towards Ploërmel. About 3 km beyond the D775 turn-off a road leads left to the partly ruined Largoët Castle, known as the 'Elven Towers'. The massive 57-m-high octagonal keep was built in the 14th c. On summer evenings the castle is used as a stage set for theatre productions.

Crévy comes next, located further along the N166 just beyond the little town of La Chapelle. Its 14th c. military architecture conceals its 3rd c. origins. Inside is a museum of costumes from the period 1730 to 1975.

Trécesson: From Ploërmel follow the N24 east to Campénéac and from there the D32 to the castle. The late medieval building nestling idyllically in the valley casts its reflection on the waters of an artificial lake. The castle is not open to the public. *Ploërmel* itself – to which you then return – offers its own rewards in the shape of the lovely old houses in the Rue Beaumanoir and the interesting church of St-Armel.

Suscinio Castle

The château, Josselin

Pardon at Josselin

Josselin: Turn off the N24 (westbound) for Josselin. The little town developed as early as the 6th c. around its fortress-like defences above the River Oust. With its solid towers and glorious façade, the present château moves the onlooker to wonder at its Late Gothic and Renaissance architecture. Inside is an exhibition of some 500 dolls from the Rohan collection. The basilica church of Notre-Dame-du-Roncier is largely Late Gothic.

Guéhenno: 4.5 km west of Josselin, along the N24, the D778 branches off to Guéhenno which boasts the only calvary in the whole of Morbihan. Quite exceptional in the beauty of its composition, the calvary was almost destroyed in the French Revolution and rebuilt in the 19th c. with some alterations and with new sculptures.

Pontivy: Return towards Josselin and take the D764 to Pontivy where the *Rohan castle* dominates the Old Town. The castle walls, 3 m thick and 18–20 m high, bear witness to the great power of the Rohan family in those days. In addition to the music festivals held here in the summer there is a continuous programme of special exhibitions.

(Most of the castles are open from spring to autumn. Pontivy stays open throughout the year while Lehélec is only open in July and August.)

In search of the Stone Age — dolmens and menhirs

Auray Pop. 9,000

This small town is famous mainly for the Battle of Auray (1364) which brought the Breton War of Succession to an end. Worth visiting are the old 15th and 17th c. houses, the picturesque Quartier St-Goustan, and the church of St-Gildas (17th c.).

 Very pleasant paths along the River Loch.

Harbour for pleasure-craft.

 6 km north-east is *Ste-Anne-d'Auray*, the best-known place of pilgrimage in Brittany ever since the appearance there of St Anne in 1623. Pilgrimages begin at Easter and continue until the first Sunday in October (they are held regularly on Wednesdays and Sundays from May 1st to July 10th). The high points of the year are the St Anne Pardon (July 26th) and the Rosary Pardon (August 25th) when Bretons from all over the region gather dressed in their local costumes.

Locmariaquer

From Auray the D28 leads south to Locmariaquer, famous for its megalithic monuments. The Mané Rethual dolmen stands in the centre of the town itself. The Grand Menhir – Brittany's largest, 20.3 m long – lies on the ground broken into four pieces. Not far away is the dolmen known as the Merchants' Table (Table des Marchands), which has some interesting engravings on the rear supporting stone. The uprights of the Mané Lud dolmen are also decorated with engravings. Carry on beyond Locmariaquer to the *Pointe de Kerpenhir* to enjoy the splendid view and to visit the *Allée Couverte des Pierres Plates*.

Leave the Locmariaquer peninsula by the D781 and head west. From the Kérisper bridge a wonderful view unfolds of the Crach estuary and the magnificent yacht harbour at *La Trinité-sur-Mer*. This one-time fishing village (noted for its oyster-beds) has developed into a thriving bathing resort and internationally famous regatta centre.

L'Azimut, 1 Rue du Men-Da: lobster grilled over a wood fire.

Gavrinis

Boats leave several times a day from Larmor-Baden on the Golfe du Morbihan for one of the most impressive of all megalithic burial mounds, the Gavrinis Tumulus (3500 BC). The structure, almost 8 m high and with a circumference of 100 m, is situated on a small hillock on the uninhabited island of Gavrinis ('Goat Island'). A 14-m-deep gallery with twenty-three supports and nine roof slabs leads to a rectangular burial chamber inside the mound. The carvings on the stone supports look rather like huge fingerprints. They are abstract designs representing the great Mother Goddess, while stone axes and serpents are also depicted.

Er Lanic

On the tiny island of Er Lanic, just south of Gavrinis, there is a double cromlech in the shape of a great figure of eight. Owing to post-glacial changes in sea-level during a period when the coast was also sinking, many of the standing stones are visible only at low tide.

Carnac Pop. 3,700

Carnac has become famous the world over for its extraordinary legacy from the period of megalithic culture. Here, on a harsh heathland not far from the sea, stand a vast number of excellently preserved stone monuments – alignments, dolmens and menhirs.

But Carnac is not just a megalithic site. It is also a beach resort, popular for its good sea-bathing and healthy air.

Carnac-Bourg with its church of St-Cornély is the old town centre. During the summer, however, life revolves round the villas and hotels of *Carnac-Plage* which offers everything for a perfect beach holiday. Sheltered in the lee of the *Quiberon* Peninsula it has a number of gently sloping sandy beaches,

Carnac

safe at all states of the tide. Its waters are warmed by a nearby sea current and its climate is mild, with Mediterranean-type plants (mimosa, evergreen oaks) to be found amongst the Atlantic stone-pine and cypress woods.

Musée de Préhistoire J. Miln-Z. Le Rouzic

The museum of prehistory is in the Place de la Chapelle, Carnac-Bourg. With its modern, outstandingly well-presented and informative exhibition of the grave-sites and settlements of the megalithic period it is among the best of its kind in the world. On display are finds from excavations in the Carnac area dating from 4000 BC to the 8th c. AD. (Open all year.)

St-Michel Tumulus

The St-Michel Tumulus is the symbol of Carnac-Bourg. It is a royal burial mound

10 m high, 125 m long and 60 m wide, with two burial chambers and twenty smaller chambered graves covered with earth. In 1664 the chapel of St-Michel was built on its flat top.

     18-hole course.

 Fête des menhirs (festival of the menhirs), third Sun. in August.

 Thalassotherapy.

La Marine, 4 Place de la Chapelle: devilfish, fish soup; *Belle Epoque*: a thirties-style restaurant offering stuffed mussels, fish; *Lan Roz*: fish specialities. The seafood here is served on seaweed.

Tour of the alignments

The route is signposted as the 'Circuit des Alignements'. The lines, kilometres long, begin at the north end of Carnac. About 3,000 menhirs and numerous dolmens are concentrated here. Around the Golfe du Morbihan alone there are twelve alignments of which the Le Ménec, Kermario and Kerlescan lines – with a combined length of 4 km – are considered the most spectacular.

In the *Alignements du Ménec* a total of 1,099 menhirs are arranged in 11 parallel rows, their heights varying from 60 cm to 4 m. At each end the alignment terminates in a semicircular cromlech. Because in the past many stones have been removed for building purposes the alignments are not all complete.

The *Alignements de Kermario* extend for 1,120 m, the rows being composed of 1,029 menhirs in all. Those at the west end are up to 6 m in height. The tower of a half-derelict mill roughly in the centre of the alignments provides an excellent vantage-point from which to survey the whole army of stones. The rows of menhirs pass right over the *Manio-Kermario* long grave, proving that the latter already existed before the menhirs were erected. Beyond the alignments a road branching off to the right from the D196 leads to the castle of Kercado. Nearby is the *Kercado* tumulus (3800 BC), on top of which stands a small menhir. The 6-m-long gallery of the tumulus ends in a burial chamber formed by six upright stones (some engraved) supporting a gigantic roof slab.

The *Alignements de Kerlescan* are only a little further along the D196. Here 555 menhirs stand in rows 880 m long. Forming a continuation of them are the *Petit Ménec* alignments, in which a total of 101 stones in 7 rows terminate in a cromlech. As you turn left at the junction of the D186 and D768 and return towards Carnac there are more mega-

lithic monuments to be seen: the *Moustoir* and *Crucuny* tumuli, the *Keriaval* dolmen, and three gallery graves known as the *Mané Kerioned* (the Dwarves' House).

The area between Plouharnel and the River Etal is also rich in megaliths. Of special note are the *Crucuno* dolmen and the *Kerzhero* alignments (1,100 menhirs in 2-km-long rows).

The Quiberon Peninsula

Once an island, Quiberon is connected to the mainland by a strip of dunes narrowing to only 100 m wide. Running due north and south the peninsula enjoys the advantages of two very contrasting stretches of coastline. The east side with its many beaches encircles Quiberon Bay, offering ideal conditions for bathing as well as all kinds of watersports. *St-Pierre-Quiberon* is a small seaside resort of just 2,000 inhabitants. It has a cromlech and alignment which warrant a visit.

The west side on the other hand, the *Côte Sauvage* or 'wild coast', is dominated by high, steep rocky cliffs gnawed by the Atlantic into caves and natural arches (at Pont-Blanc). Right to its very southernmost tip at Pointe du Conguel it is continually exposed to the breakers. The currents and heavy surf prohibit bathing on this stretch of the coast so that here, where vegetation is defeated by the searing wind and little manages to maintain a foothold in the soil, people enjoy the countryside by walking, cycling or riding.

Quiberon (pop. 4,800) is the largest town on the peninsula. In 1924 this little holiday centre was classified as a thermal spa and health resort. There is a direct train connection to Paris.

The Côte Sauvage, Quiberon Peninsula

  Yacht harbour, marine aquarium.

  Thalassotherapy.

 From Quiberon there are ferries to the offshore islands to the south (see below).

Houat and Hoëdic: 6,600 years ago these were a single island until the post-

Belle-Île-en-Mer

glacial rise in sea-level (about 10 m) separated them. Burial finds indicate the existence of Stone Age settlements here.

Belle-Île-en-Mer, largest of Brittany's Atlantic islands

The 'Beautiful Isle', 17 km long and varying between 5 and 10 km in width, does more than justice to its name. It can be reached by sea or by air from Quiberon (the car-ferry takes one hour). As on the Quiberon Peninsula the west coast (Côte Sauvage) is deeply fissured with rugged headlands, rock pinnacles and stacks, while on the leeward side of the island there are splendid sandy beaches. Between extensive tracts of heathland little whitewashed houses crouch among fertile fields.

Le Palais, midway along the sheltered north-east side, is Belle-Île's main town. Here buses wait to take day-trippers on a round tour. Alternatively the island can be explored on a hired bicycle. The town's finest landmark is its massive citadel, constructed in 1549 on the orders of Henri II. Inside is a small museum containing fascinating documents on the island's history.

 Discovering the island

The *Grand Phare*, in the south-west corner, is the most powerful lighthouse in France. From its balcony there is a tremendous panorama. Nearby *Port-Goulphar* with its small harbour (fishing and sailing craft) is the most enchanting place on Belle-Île. The Port-Coton *Aiguilles* (Needles) are part of a marvellous natural landscape created by the sea. In the *Grotte de l'Apothicairerie* (Apothecary's Cave) abandoned cormorants' nests look like chemists' jars – hence the name. And from the lighthouse on the *Pointe des Poulains* there is another superb panoramic view which includes the little yacht-filled harbour at *Sauzon*.

West Morbihan

Lorient Pop. 70,000

In the 17th c. this town in west Morbihan was developed by Louis XIV's chief minister Colbert as the base for an East India trading company, which is how it acquired its name, L'Orient (the Orient). Having been badly damaged in the War Lorient has been rebuilt as a modern city, its economic life revolving round its shipyards, the submarine base, the commercial harbour and the Keroman 'Port de Pêche' (fish dock).

 To the Île de Groix (45-minute crossing).

Hennebont Pop. 12,500

Hennebont lies at the head of the Blavet estuary and is now almost merged with Lorient. The town and the old walls around the Ville Close were destroyed towards the end of the War, but the 15th c. *Porte du Broërec* gate, with its two round towers, and the church of *Notre-Dame-du-Paradis*, which has a lovely Flamboyant porch, survived the bombing. The Hennebont stud-farm (Rue Victor Hugo) – in the grounds of the former *Abbaye de la Joie Notre-Dame*, founded by Cistercians in the 13th c. – is open to visitors.

 Château de Locguénole: Breton specialities.

A trip into the Middle Ages

For those who are interested in the ecclesiastical art of Brittany mention must be made of the impressive Flamboyant Gothic chapel in the little town of *Kernascléden*, some distance north of Hennebont. In addition to a wealth of sculptural ornamentation the chapel is decorated with 15th c. frescos including a Dance of Death. In *St-Fiacre* – a Late Gothic chapel 13 km further west near Le Faouët – there is another wonderful masterpiece: an intricately carved rood screen in the Flamboyant style. The marvellously expressive figures of Christ and the two thieves are especially worth noting. Three more churches worth visiting are *Ste-Barbe* which stands in a lovely rural setting, *St-Nicolas* which has a fine wooden rood screen illustrating the story of the saint, and the *Abbaye de Langonnet*, rebuilt in the 17th and 18th c. but with a 13th c. chapter-house.

Calvary at Melrand

Calvary at Plougastel-Daoulas

Finistère: land of calvaries

In the Stone Age Finistère was believed to be the limit of the inhabited world, the 'land at the end of the earth' (Finis Terrae). Westward the sun sank into the sea, and this for these early peoples was the frontier of the Beyond whence the souls of the dead migrated. The present-day Finistère department is without fashionable tourist resorts. Instead it has a breathtaking natural beauty, nowhere more strikingly in evidence than at the *Pointe du Raz*. The *rias* (river valleys flooded by the sea) which cut deep inland, called 'Aber' (as in l'Aber-Wrac'h) in the northern part and 'Aven' (as in Pont-Aven) in the south, are characteristic of the Finistère coastline, while equally characteristic of the interior are the chequerboard landscape of hedged fields and the rugged heights such as Roc-Trévezel (384 m) in the Monts d'Arrée and Ménez-Hom (330 m) in the Montagnes Noires. But there is a great deal more to Finistère than just its wonderful scenery. It is also a living history-book.

Quimper Pop. 60,500

Quimper, one-time capital of the Duchy of Cornouaille and now chief town of the Finistère department, has grown up in an exceptionally pretty location where the River Steir flows into the Odet. Its name, Breton of course, comes from the word *kemper* meaning confluence. A couple of kilometres south of the town, where the Odet widens out like a lake, is Quimper's port. From there the now tidal river flows a further 16 km through gentle, green countryside before spilling out into the Atlantic near Bénodet.

West doorway, Quimper Cathedral

Quimper

From the 70-m-high vantage-point of *Mont Frugy* on the left bank of the river there is a fine view of Quimper's delightful setting. The town is busy but has managed to retain its traditional Breton atmosphere. Until the French Revolution Quimper was also known as Corentin, after the first bishop to be appointed to the bishopric created by King Gradlon (see page 16).

 A walk through the town

There are beautiful half-timbered houses in the Rue Kéréon, Rue Guéodet, Rue Elie Fréron, Rue St-Mathieu and Rue du Sallé.

The Cathédrale St-Corentin with its 76-m-high spire is the dominant building in the Old Town. It is situated in the Place St-Corentin which is also graced by a monument to Quimper's most celebrated son, the doctor Laënnec. Gothic in style, the cathedral was founded in 1240. The neo-Gothic spires were added between 1854 and 1856, the architects having been influenced by the church in nearby Pont-Croix. Between the spires there is an equestrian statue of King Gradlon.

The cathedral is entered through the richly decorated west doorway. The ground-plan is interesting because the chancel is not aligned with the nave, suggesting perhaps some difficulties with the foundations. Particularly fine 15th c. stained-glass windows adorn the galleries in the nave and transept. There is also a fine 15th c. alabaster statue of St John.

Museums: Immediately south of the cathedral in the Rue Gradlon stands the museum of local history, the *Musée Départemental Breton*, which provides an excellent insight into Breton home life and folk art. In the same square, right next to the Hôtel de Ville (town hall), is the *Musée des Beaux-Arts* (museum of fine art) with a collection of French and foreign paintings.

The potteries: The pottery workshops or *faïenceries* (open to the public) in the suburb of Locmaria were established in the 17th c. The patterns used to decorate the ceramics are a distinctive blend of influences from Moustier, Nevers and Rouen as well as the Orient.

 Bar Breton, 18 Rue de Frout: popular with young people; *La Tour d'Auvergne*, 13 Rue des Réguaires: salmon, mussels, shrimps and prawns.

 Grandes Fêtes de Cornouaille, held annually on the fourth Sunday in July: Breton music – harp and *biniou* (bagpipes) – and folk-dancing, theatre, costume parade and celebration of local cuisine.

Ex **North of Quimper – a short tour by car**

First stop on the drive of about 30 km is the 15th c. chapel at *Kerdévot* with its famous Flemish altarpiece. Next comes the *Site de Stangala*, a stunning natural monument from where there is a delightful view of the valley of the Odet far below. The final ports of call are *Notre-Dame-de-Quilinen* and *St-Venec*, two chapels possessing particularly interesting and unusual calvaries (both 16th c., and similar in composition).

South Finistère from Bénodet to Quimperlé

By boat from Quimper to Bénodet: The excursion down the River Odet takes one and a half hours, departure times depending on the tides. After passing through the lake-like Baie de Kérogan the river narrows again and begins to meander. The boat slips past rocks known as the *Maiden's Leap* and *Bishop's Chair* and on downstream, past the ruins of Roman baths on the right bank near Perennou, to Bénodet.

Bénodet: The scenery along the river culminates delightfully in the white sandy beaches and busy marina at Bénodet, where from the Pyramide lighthouse there is a grand view over the town and along the coast as far as the Îles de Glénan.

Another splendid vista is gained from the 30-m-high *Cornouaille Bridge* which crosses the Odet just 1 km to the northwest. At *Le Drennec*, some 5 km northeast, the chapel's 16th c. fountain has a gable decorated in a crocket motif.

    Thalassotherapy.

Fouesnant: This little holiday town is encircled by orchards, mostly of apple-trees the fruit from which is pressed to make the delicious Breton cider. The Romanesque church was built in the 12th c. but altered in the 18th, while its calvary dates from the 17th c. Renowned and especially lovely are the Fouesnant costumes and head-dresses, now seldom worn except at the *Pardon Ste-Anne* on the first Sunday after July 26th.

Beg-Meil: This seaside resort sits astride the point – 'Mill Point' is how the Breton name translates – at the south-western tip of the Baie de la Forêt. During the summer months there are crossings to Concarneau on the opposite side of the bay.

La Forêt-Fouesnant: Situated some 3.5 km east of Fouesnant this little place, hidden amongst greenery, offers a relaxing holiday and excellent sports facilities including a yacht harbour at Port-la-Forêt. Boat trips are run from here to the River Odet and across to the Îles de Glénan.

 Auberge du sous bois, Route de Pont Lorois.

Concarneau Pop. 19,000

This popular resort on the Baie de la Forêt is blessed with extremely pleasant beaches and a fine marina. It is also the third most important fishing port in France, the tuna catch here being the country's largest. The fishmarket is a bustling, colourful spectacle. Much of the fish brought into the port is processed by the canneries in the town.

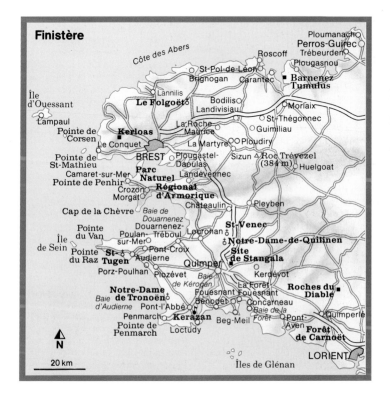

Concarneau and its inner harbour

Apart from that of St-Malo, Concarneau's walled Old Town, whose ramparts were renewed in the 16th c., is the best surviving example of a Ville Close. It is built on a small island 350 m long by 100 m wide, and entered via a fortification linked to the island and mainland by bridges on either side. Within the walls, in the Rue Vauban, the old arsenal has been turned into the *Musée de la Pêche* (fishing museum), which tells the story of the town's history as well as of the development of the port, shipbuilding, navigation, the traditional fishing industry and deep-sea fishing. The *Laboratoire Maritime* of the Collège de France on the Quai de la Croix has an exhibition on the marine environment.

 La Gallandière, 3 Place G. de Gaulle: smoked salmon, spiny lobster au gratin; *L'Océan*, Plage des sables blancs: panoramic view.

 Fêtes des Filets bleus: sardine-fishermen's festival on the last Sunday in August.

Pont-Aven Pop. 3,500

This village at the mouth of the Aven is exceptionally lovely. The songwriter Théodore Botrel sang the praises of its ancient watermills, and it was he who established the Gorse Bloom Festival which takes place every year on the first Sunday in August.

 The Pont-Aven School

Pont-Aven is most widely known for the school of painting to which it has given its name. Artists such as Paul Sérusier, Emile Bernard, Emile Schuffenecker and Charles Laval were among the many painters who in the late 19th c. sought new inspiration by coming here, forsaking 'civilisation' for this rural landscape with its air of melancholy and its simple style of life. By far the most famous was Paul Gauguin (1848–1903) who later left France altogether, carrying his search for the primitive to the South Seas where his artistry reached new heights. The works of some of the Pont-Aven artists are on display in the *Musée de la Ville* though unfortunately Gauguin is not represented, his paintings having been dispersed throughout the world's great museums. Although the painter lived in the South Seas from 1895 to the end of his life, his last painting, *Breton Village in Winter*, re-invoked memories of Brittany.

There is a round walk along the banks of the Aven and through the *Bois d'Amour* (Lovers' Wood). Signposts mark the places which particularly inspired the painters. It was the crucifix in the chapel at *Trémalo*, a simple 16th c. country church, which moved Gauguin to paint his famous *Yellow Christ*.

Quimperlé Pop. 11,700

This small holiday town east of Pont-Aven is attractively situated at the confluence of the Rivers Ellé and Isole. These merge to form the Laïta which then flows into the sea at Le Pouldu. Quimperlé's lower town clusters around the 12th c. abbey church of *Ste-Croix*, which was rebuilt between 1864 and

Quimperlé

1868 after the tower had collapsed causing much devastation. Considerable care was taken to keep faithfully to the original, a circular building with three apsidal chapels and porch. Of special interest are the Romanesque apse, a stone retable from the Renaissance period, and the crypt, which possesses some superb capitals. Lovely old houses still line the Rue Ellé, the Rue

Pont-Aven

Quimperlé

Traditional Bigouden costume

Pont-l'Abbé

Brémond-d'Ars and the Rue Dom-Morice, where a local museum is housed in the 15th c. *Maison des Archers* (Archers' House), an old half-timbered building with projecting upper storeys. The less ancient upper town is centred round the church of *Notre-Dame-de-l'Assomption* (13th and 15th c.) which has a richly ornamented porch.

  　　Freshwater angling.

Ex Two country excursions

Highly recommended are two short excursions into the country from Quimperlé. Some 12 km north-east are *Les Roches du Diable* (Devil's rocks), a sea of stone on the banks of the Ellé. About 5 km south of Quimperlé is the oak and beech wood of *Carnoët*, shrouded in legend and offering some lovely walks.

Pays Bigouden

The Penmarch Peninsula between the Odet estuary and the Baie d'Audierne is known as the Bigouden – the name coming from the tall, unicorn-like lace head-dresses worn by the women of the region. As well as megaliths and medieval churches the Bigouden is a land of calvaries, and constitutes a truly worthwhile excursion from Quimper.

Pont-l'Abbé Pop. 8,000

This, the main town in the Bigouden, straddling the mouth of the little River Abbé, is nowadays a bustling shopping centre. But the traditional arts of bobbin lacemaking, embroidery and Breton furniture-making for which the town is famous are still very much alive. In the partly medieval castle (14th and 18th c.) the *Musée Bigouden* has collections of furniture, costumes and model ships.

Fête des Brodeuses: embroiderers' festival on the second Sunday in July.

Around Pont-l'Abbé

The chapel of *Notre-Dame-de-Tréminou* (14th and 16th c.) and the Gothic church of *St-Jean-Trolimon* are both worth visiting.

Notre-Dame-de-Tronoën:

Alongside the chapel of Notre-Dame-de-Tronoën, which stands amid lonely sand dunes about 3 km west of Pont-l'Abbé, is the oldest and most remarkable of all the Breton calvaries, carved between 1450 and 1460. In contrast to those of later calvaries its figures lean against the rear of their stone block, many being bas-reliefs and only a few of them free-standing.

Penmarch

to the south is a district which includes a number of separate villages – St-Guénolé, Kerity, Tréoultré and St-Pierre. Its houses cling to a wild and windswept stretch of coast punctuated at intervals by rocky headlands. The Penmarch Peninsula was very prosperous until the 16th c., owing to the wealth generated by cod-fishing in the surrounding waters. But the disappearance of the shoals, together with piracy and severe floods, brought a sudden end to its prosperity.

In the *Musée Préhistorique Finistérien,* 1 km outside Penmarch on the road north-west, are exhibits from the Stone Age to Gallo-Roman times (open June to September).

The Eckmühl lighthouse

with a range of 54 km towers 65 m above Cap Penmarch. From the top it is possible to see as far as the Pointe du Raz (the next peninsula to the north) with the Île de Sein offshore, eastwards to Concarneau, and seawards to the Îles de Glénan. It is a breathtaking vantage-point.

Loctudy:

This little port and seaside resort lies to the east of Penmarch on the Abbé estuary, facing the island of Tudy. Its 12th c. church is the best-preserved Romanesque building in Brittany, though the façade and belfry date from the 18th c. The four columns in the chancel have Romanesque capitals with foliage decoration.

Kerazan Château,

set in parkland outside Loctudy (in the direction of Pont-l'Abbé), is open to the public. Its rooms, in Louis Quinze style, are hung with paintings from the 15th c. to the modern period. The Flemish and Dutch schools are particularly well represented.

The far west of Finistère

Quimper to the Pointe du Raz

Take the D784 to *Plozévet*, centre of a country and coastal district midway along the Baie d'Audierne and on the boundary of the Pays Bigouden. Its Gothic church is built on Romanesque foundations laid in the 13th c. A rewarding detour then takes you to the chapels of La Trinité, St-Démet and St-Renan.

Just 1 km further on is the small fishing village of *Porz-Poulhan* overlooking the Baie d'Audierne.

 Au Roi Gradlon: its speciality is grilled lobster with tarragon sauce.

Pont-Croix, 5.5 km north-east of Audierne, remains very unspoilt. Its church,

Pointe du Van

Notre-Dame-de-Roscudon, has a Romanesque nave. It also possesses a side chapel with especially fine stained-glass windows (1540) and a Gothic porch built in the 14th c. Further west, branching left off the D784 to Pointe du Raz, a road leads to the chapel of *St-Tugen* (16th and 17th c.) where a pardon is held every year on the Saturday and Sunday before the feast of St John (June 24th).

Pointe du Raz

There can be few pieces of coastline as spectacular as the Pointe du Raz, the most westerly point in Brittany and indeed in France. To stand on these rocky cliffs pounded by foaming waves is definitely one of the highlights of any trip to Brittany. In the foreground squats the flat Île de Sein beyond which, in clear weather, the Ar Men lighthouse, and north-west of that the Tévennec lighthouse, both on rocky islets, can just be made out.

For the sure-footed the one-and-a-half-hour walk round the point is an experience not to be missed. But you will need non-slip footwear. (It is possible to hire a guide.)

Île de Sein

A mere 800 people live on the island, so poor that they are still exempt from paying taxes. Their houses huddle together for protection against the weather. There is evidence to suggest that the island was once bigger and has lost much of its former area to the destructive action of the breakers. Twice in the last century it was completely overwhelmed by tidal waves.

At one time the islanders were notorious for piracy. In truth the unusually fierce currents of the Raz-de-Sein left many a ship stranded in heavy weather. Any survivors were ruthlessly killed and the wrecks plundered. In the 19th c. this savagery was halted and the islanders turned to saving lives instead of ending them.

In summer a boat runs three times a day linking the island with Audierne (once a day for the rest of the year).

Pointe du Van

Between the Pointe du Raz and Pointe du Van – the headland immediately to the north – is the *Baie des Trépassés* or Bay of the Departed, said to have got its name from the many bodies washed ashore there from foundered ships. The Pointe du Van itself is crowned by the 15th c. chapel of *St-They* and affords a wide vista right the way from the Pointe du Raz to the Pointe de Castelmeur, Pointe de Brézellec, Cap de la Chèvre, Pointe de Penhir and Pointe de St-Mathieu.

The Baie de Douarnenez

Between Pointe du Van and Douarnenez the steep rocky coastline with headlands (such as the Pointe de Brézellec) jutting out seawards at intervals offers a series of views each as superb as the other. A visit to the bird sanctuary at Cap Sizun adds further to the pleasure,

especially during the nesting season between March and May.

At Poullan-sur-Mer a road branching off south leads to two chapels, Notre-Dame-de-Kérinec (13th and 15th c.) and Notre-Dame-de-Confort (16th c.). Each is well worth the detour.

Douarnenez-Tréboul Pop. 20,000

Douarnenez, Ploaré, Pouldavid and Tréboul, once four small separate communities, have merged to form a single town straddling the little River Pouldavid on one of the loveliest bays in Brittany.

Douarnenez is a busy fishing port, earning its living primarily from catching and canning fish. Following the construction of the Nouveau Port the small harbour at Rosmeur is now used mainly by sardine-boats. You should make a point of going to see the colourful fish auction.

Just offshore at the mouth of the river is the Île Tristan, by tradition associated with the tragic lovers Tristan and Isolde.

Tréboul on the left bank of the Pouldavid is a popular resort with yacht harbour and sailing school.

Starting from the Port du Rosmeur there is a very pleasant walk along the *Sentier de Plomarc'hs* with views of the town, harbour and bay.

 Thalassotherapy.

Locronan Pop. 700

This little village owes its name to an Irishman, St Ronan, who came and lived here as a recluse. He taught the villagers to weave and so brought them prosperity, a prosperity to which the beautiful village square bears witness even today. On it stand the church of *St-Ronan* (15th c.) and the adjoining

Douarnenez

Pénity chapel (16th c.) which contains the saint's tomb – watched over by a statue of St Michael dating from about 1430. Also inside are a pulpit with scenes from the life of St Ronan, and 15th c. stained glass. The *Ateliers St-Ronan* and *Ronan Pré* are linen-weaving workshops with exhibition rooms and a craft shop.

Every year on the second Sunday in July St Ronan is honoured in a pardon called the *Petite Troménie*, while every sixth year (1989, 1995) a *Grande Troménie* is held. However, the most delightful of all Brittany's pardons takes place not here but at the neighbouring *Ste-Anne-la-Palud*, on the last Sunday in August. The pilgrims' village of tents and booths is a picturesque bustle of activity.

Le fer à cheval, Place de l'Eglise: Renaissance building; *Du Prieuré*, 11 Rue du Prieuré.

The Armorique Regional Nature Park

The Armorique nature park extends over about 105,000 hectares and encompasses more than 25 of Finis-tère's rural communities, with a total population of more than 48,000. It includes areas of coast (the Crozon Peninsula and Aulne estuary) and also islands (the Ouessant group and the Île de Sein) as well as the Monts d'Arrée region inland which boasts Brittany's highest peak, the 384-m Roc Trévezel. The nature park is regionally administered and much effort has gone into creating a point of introduction to the country-side for the town-dweller, a place of escape and relaxation where people can both experience and study their environment and the natural world.

A park full of unusual museums

Very popular with horse-lovers is Britta-ny's *Museum of the Horse* in Hanvec, on the Ménez-Meur estate between Sizun and Le Faou. At *Kerouat* – situated in a little valley between Commana and Sizun – you can learn about the history of the village and visit the mills and miller's house. South-east of Sizun the *Maison Cornec* in St-Rivoal typifies the style of building in the Pays de Léon between the 17th and 19th c. On the Drénnec dam, again south-east of Sizun, the *River House* contains a museum devoted to rivers and freshwater angling. North-east of Huelgoat the old railway station at Scrignac-Berrien is now home to a *hunting museum*. On the return west the *Philhaouers Museum*, in the old presbytery at Loqueffret on the D14 between Huelgoat and Lannédern, details the history of the semi-nomadic former inhabitants of the Monts d'Arrée. Below Montagne St-Michel, in the Ferme St-Michel at Brasparts, the *Maison des Artisans* has a permanent exhibition of art and craftwork. Further west still the *Maison des Minéraux* (mineral museum) in St-Hernot – *en route* to Cap de la Chèvre on the Crozon Peninsula – lays on guided tours of the Armorican chain for those interested in the geology of the area. Brittany's college of agriculture in Trégarvan, south-east of Landévennec, incorporates the *Musée de l'Ecole Rurale*, while at Landévennec itself there is the *abbey museum* (open throughout the year). On Ouessant there are two interesting museums, one in the *Maison du Niou Huella* illustrating island life, the other at *Créac'h lighthouse* devoted to the history of maritime lights and signals. (Most museums are open between June and September. For information tel. 98 68 81 71.)

Châteaulin

Châteaulin (pop. 5,700) is famous for its salmon-fishing. Nestling in the narrow valley of the Aulne its ruined castle and 15th c. chapel of *Notre-Dame* (sheltering within the walls of the parish close) are well worth a visit.

As you drive west from Châteaulin a road to the right off the D887 leads to the 330-m-high *Ménez-Hom*, one of the best vantage-points in Brittany. Continuing in the direction of Crozon you come to a left turn (D108) to the chapels of *St-Nic* and *St-Côme*.

The Crozon Peninsula

Taking its name from the small town of *Crozon* (pop. 8,000) this deeply indented peninsula, about 30 km in length, is an area of supreme natural beauty. The mild climate also makes it ideally suited to growing vegetables. The excursion by boat from *Morgat* to the *Grandes Grottes* (Great Caves) is well worth making. The *Petites Grottes* (Little Caves) are accessible only at low tide.

From Morgat it is barely 8 km to *Cap de la Chèvre* and yet another impressive coastal panorama. Equally fine coastal views are obtained from the *Pointe de Dinan* (where there is a rock formation known as the *Château de Dinan*), the *Pointe de Penhir* (with the *Tas de Pois* rocks just off the tip – the name means 'pile of peas') and the *Pointe des Espagnols*. Noted for its spiny lobsters *Camaret-sur-Mer* is both fishing village and quiet, unsophisticated beach resort. *Landévennec* occupies an especially lovely situation at the mouth of the Aulne. The new Benedictine abbey there (1958) opens its doors to visitors, and the carefully restored ruins of the old abbey can also be explored.

Pleyben

Pleyben (pop. 4,000), to the south-east, also lies well within the boundary of the Regional Nature Park. The calvary inside the walled parish close (mid-16th to 17th c.) is one of the most interesting in Brittany. Above the nave of Pleyben's church rise two towers, one of them a Renaissance structure crowned by a dome and lantern.

There is another impressive 16th c. parish close at *Brasparts*. If you head further east via Lannédern and Loqueffret a detour left will take you to the *Centrale Nucléaire des Monts d'Arrée* (nuclear power station) and the *St-Michel* reservoir before you continue through St-Herbot to Huelgoat.

Huelgoat (pop. 2,300) has a Late Gothic church with a superb choir screen. Huelgoat is one of the most popular inland resorts in Brittany, being blessed with great natural beauty: wooded hills, a lake, streams and fascinating rock formations. Picturesque paths wend their way through the woods to the rocks – le Chaos du Moulin, la Grotte du Diable and the wobbly Roche Tremblante – as well as to the Grotte d'Artus (cave) and the Camp d'Artus, a Gallo-Roman encampment.

Brest and the Côte des Abers
Brest Pop. 172,000

The city stands on the northern side of the sheltered *Rade de Brest*, a magnificent natural harbour linked to the open sea by the narrow *Goulet de Brest*, only 2 km wide. The excellence of its position was well appreciated by the Romans, who used it as a base. In the 14th c. Brest came under English rule, possession being regained for France by Charles VI in 1397. In the 18th c. the city underwent a period of rapid expansion during which the arsenals and dockyard were constructed and a number of maritime schools established. Having been almost completely destroyed in the Second World War the rebuilt Brest,

modern in appearance and geometrically laid out, has the unmistakable air of a town created from the drawing-board. Commercial and industrial sectors make it economically one of Brittany's most dynamic centres, and it is also the region's second largest university city. The Port de Guerre, started in the 17th c., is today the biggest naval base in France, capable of handling warships of every size.

 Sightseeing in the port

The harbour: From the Cours Dajot promenade there is a fine view out over the Rade de Brest and over the city and commercial port below. Tours of the harbour lasting about half an hour are run between April and September.

Château: At the western end of the Cours Dajot stands Brest's sole surviving monument from the past, the château (12th and 17th c.), which stands on Roman foundations dating from AD 310. The perimeter walls were restored following the Second World War. The castle is now the home of the Marine Prefecture, while its east wing has been turned into a *naval museum* (Musée Naval) housing a collection of model ships and old sea charts.

The Musée Municipal (city museum) in the Rue Traverse has a collection of French, Italian and Flemish paintings as well as works by artists of the Pont-Aven School (see page 60).

 Les Antilles, 12 Rue de Siam: fish specialities, seafood served on seaweed.

Link via Le Conquet to the Île d'Ouessant.

The calvary at Plougastel-Daoulas – detail

Around Brest
The Plougastel Peninsula south-east of Brest is reached by way of the Pont Albert-Louppe spanning the River Elorn. The small town of *Plougastel-Daoulas* lies at the heart of Brittany's main strawberry-growing area. The calvary there – it has more than 180 figures, carved between 1602 and 1604 – is well worth going to see. No less interesting is the 12th c. Romanesque church in neighbouring Daoulas, with its carved fountain and elegant cloister in the abbey garden. From there it is just a few minutes' walk to the chapel of Notre-Dame-des-Fontaines and another fountain (1532) which stands beside it.

Pointe de St-Mathieu: If you drive westwards from Brest on the D789 a number of short detours lead to various vantage-points from which to enjoy beautiful views along the coast as far as the Pointe de St-Mathieu (impressive cliffs). The lighthouse on the Pointe (open to the public) has a range of 55 to 60 km. Nearby are the romantic ruins of a 13th c. Gothic abbey church.

Le Conquet just 4 km to the north is a small resort where the fishermen specialise in catching spiny lobster, lobster, crab and spider crab. There are daily crossings to Ouessant calling in at the tiny island of Molène.

Île d'Ouessant (English: Ushant)
This sea-girt westernmost extremity of Brittany, 7 km by 4 km in area, is inhabited by barely 2,000 people. Since 1969 it has been part of the Parc Naturel Régional d'Armorique (see page 66). Frequent storms rage over its rocky coast and fog reduces visibility almost to zero. So Ouessant's reefs have long

been notorious for the number of ships coming to grief there. The island is almost entirely given over to sheep grazing. Traditional costume and ancient customs survive better here than elsewhere.

Proëlle means the homecoming of souls. It is the name of a burial ceremony performed on the island when mariners or fishermen are believed lost at sea. The missing person is represented by a wax cross which is laid to rest in a kind of mausoleum in the cemetery at Lampaul, the island's 'capital'.

The day-trip by boat allows ample time for exploring the island either by bus or on hired bicycle. A museum of island life has been created in two old houses at Niou.

  　Horse-drawn cabs.

The Côte des Abers

Back on the mainland the drive north and then east from Le Conquet follows the line of the Côte des Abers, the 'coast of wide estuaries'. To date this particular stretch of the Brittany coast from the Pointe de Corsen to the seaside resort of Brignogan-Plage has largely been spared from the tourist throng. It is a typical *ria* coastline, the result of the invasion of former river valleys by the sea. Depending on the state of the tide the wide estuaries are either flooded or dry. From west to east the rias are *Aber-Ildut* (named after a Gallic saint), the enchanting *Aber-Benoît*, and *Aber-Wrac'h* (the witch's estuary). Aber-Wrac'h is the longest of the three (10 km).

The coastline here has a character all its own, being wild, isolated and only sparsely covered in vegetation. Remote bays of white sand and dunes alternate with rocky spurs of dark granite. Miles of footpaths follow the cliffs, against which the pounding waves send up plumes of spray metres high. All along the coast small roads drop down to lonely beaches where there are fine views, those on the *Ste-Marguerite* peninsula between Aber-Wrac'h and Aber-Benoît being especially lovely.

Nature at risk

In March 1978 catastrophe struck Brittany when the super-tanker *Amoco Cadiz* ran aground and broke up off Portsall. For several days thousands of tons of oil drifted ashore on the Breton coast. The whole of the north-west section between St-Mathieu and Perros-Guirec with its fishing villages and scattering of seaside resorts was heavily polluted. In all about 200 km of the Brittany coastline was contaminated. Thanks to a huge clean-up operation mounted by the military and thousands of volunteer helpers, the rocks and beaches of the bathing resorts were cleared of oil in time for the summer. But the ecological damage was considerable and some of the fishermen whose livelihoods were affected are still fighting for compensation.

The coast and its hinterland

Having visited the various small harbours such as Porspoder and Portsall, the 50-m-high cliffs of the Pointe de Corsen, and the Trézien lighthouse (open to the public, magnificent views), make a detour inland to see the 12-m-high *Kerloas* menhir, the highest still standing in Brittany. There are more menhirs and dolmens near Lannilis, 2 km north-east of which stands *Kerouartz*, a 17th c. Renaissance château.

From *Lilia* boats run to the little island of *Vierge*. Its 77-m lighthouse is the tallest in France.

Brignogan-Plage: As seaside resorts go Brignogan is small, with a population of only 1,100. But the 'Plage' part of its name promises beaches, and indeed these stretch all the way to the Pointe de Pontusval. On the edge of the village there is an interesting 'Christianised' standing stone, the Men-Marz menhir.

Le Folgoët, 12 km or so from the coast, is famous for the pilgrimage held there each September. The church of Notre-Dame has one of the finest towers in Brittany and a superb Flamboyant rood screen carved from pink granite, a masterpiece of 15th c. Breton sculpture.

The calvaries and closes of the Pays de Léon

Walled parish closes complete with calvaries, chapels and consecrated fountains are the hallmark of Finistère, their large numbers being owed to the prosperity of the cloth trade in the 16th and 17th c. This round tour of the area little more than 30 km from the coast, between the Elorn and Penze valleys, between the Léon plateau and the heights of the Monts d'Arrée, must be the architectural and artistic highlight of any visit to Brittany.

Bodilis

Bodilis is situated a few kilometres north of the Elorn valley (about 5 km from Landivisiau). Of special interest here in the parish close are the Flamboyant belfry (Léon's last Gothic church tower), the granite font, and the late 16th c. porch. The carved timbers inside the church are, together with those at Pleyben, among the finest in Finistère.

La Roche-Maurice

After leaving Bodilis drive to the D712, turning west along the romantically picturesque Elorn valley. At one time 150 watermills are reputed to have stood on its river-meadows. Continue on the D712 and then turn left for La Roche-Maurice where the ruins of a castle (c. 1060) keep watch over the valley. Here the most remarkable feature of the parish close is the charnel house or ossuary. The excellence of the sculpture on the Renaissance façade makes it the most beautiful in Brittany. Inside the church are some fine stained-glass windows (1529) and a carved oak rood screen.

La Martyre

On the way from La Roche-Maurice to La Martyre the road passes through the site of a Roman camp, which was clearly positioned here for ease of defence. The camp is believed to have covered almost 3 hectares. La Martyre itself possesses the most ancient and also the most distinctive parish close in the Pays de Léon. Already a stronghold in Gallo-Roman times (roads and an encampment), in the 14th c. the town developed into an important trading centre engaged in lively commerce with the north German and the Mediterranean ports. Despite having been built over a period stretching from the 11th to the 15th c., the various elements of the parish close – triumphal arch, calvary, charnel house and church – achieve a surprising and thoroughly satisfying harmony. The church also boasts the Léon area's oldest and most unusual porch (1455; take a close look at the sculptures, especially the depiction of the Birth of Christ, on the tympanum). In the interior of the church the carved beams, capitals, windows, and canopy over the font are all very beautiful.

Ploudiry

Next on the list to be visited is the parish close at Ploudiry, reached by taking the D35 in the direction of Landivisiau. Of interest here are the ossuary and the typical pierced Breton bell-tower (1854).

Locmélar

After Ploudiry continue on the D35 to Coasmat and then take the D30 to Le Pontic, turning left there for Locmélar. The village has one of the most charming churches in the area. Note especially the carved porch (1577). Some of Locmélar's ancient houses date back as far as the 11th c. and say much about what life was like during that period. Leave the village in the direction of Sizun.

Sizun

The parish close here is best known for its majestic late 16th c. triumphal arch. The ossuary (1585–88) has been turned into a museum. Also worth seeing are the early 16th c. Flamboyant porch and the 18th c. belfry, the latter clearly influenced by the famous belfry on the Kreisker Chapel in St-Pol-de-Léon (see page 75).

Commana

Leaving Sizun head next for Commana at the foot of the Monts d'Arrée. The church is distinguished by its Renaissance porch, its superb retable (1682) and its font. There is something else of great interest here too, reached by a short detour south of the village. This is the *allée couverte* (c. 3000 BC) at *Mougau Vihan*. The 14-m-long mass burial chamber, which quite unusually is aligned north and south, consists of sixteen uprights and five roof slabs.

Plounéour-Ménez

Leave Commana on the D764 eastwards towards Huelgoat, branching off to the right on the D11. At the junction with the D785 turn left in the direction of Morlaix. About 3 km further on is *Roc Trévezel* (384 m). Brittany's highest hill provides a stunning all-round view – northwards across a chequerboard landscape of hedged fields, and south towards the basin-shaped Brennilis valley and the St-Michel reservoir. Afterwards continue on the D785 to Plounéour-Ménez for a look at the triumphal arch and the squat houses round the church.

St-Thégonnec

The magnificent parish close, still in a perfect state of preservation, must be counted the highlight of the whole tour. St-Thégonnec was formerly one of the richest parishes in the Pays de Léon, and here more than anywhere the rivalry between neighbouring parishes – over two centuries St-Thégonnec and Guimiliau sought to outdo one another – is reflected in the splendour of its close. Before entering pause for a moment in the street to admire the triumphal arch (1587). Inside, note especially the calvary (1617), the charnel house (1676–82), the Renaissance tower (1599–1626) and the glorious carvings in the church.

Guimiliau

Follow the D712 to the crossroads at Kermat, then take the D31 to Guimiliau. A sleepy village with the squat houses typical of this area, Guimiliau boasts the second largest of all the calvaries, one on which the figures are particularly expressive. The sculpted ornamentation of the Gothic and Renaissance church porch with its vaulting and bas-reliefs is exceptionally elaborate. Inside the

church the carved oak baptistry (1675) is quite magnificent.

Lampaul-Guimiliau

From Guimiliau join the D111 to Lampaul-Guimiliau where another parish close awaits discovery, complete and perfectly preserved – triumphal arch, church, calvary, charnel house and cemetery, all within an encircling wall. The ornamentation of the church interior also includes some items of particular interest – the very fine coloured rood beam, the 17th c. canopied font, the Entombment carved from tufa (1676), a *pietà* and the magnificent 16th c. altarpieces (Flemish work, from Antwerp). The belfry steeple which was damaged by lightning in 1809 was before that one of the highest church towers in the Pays de Léon.

Landivisiau

Finally head north-west from Lampaul-Guimiliau on the D11 to Landivisiau, famous as a centre for horse-breeding – as is neighbouring Bodilis – and equally noted for its cattle market. The church of St-Thivisiau has a 16th c. porch decorated with mythological animals and human figures.

Morlaix Pop. 20,500

Morlaix, a Roman town built at the confluence of the Queffleuth and the Jarlot, lies on a stretch of the coast known as the *Ceinture Dorée* (golden belt), in the midst of one of the most important vegetable-growing areas in Brittany. The widening river estuary which runs north to the sea is commonly referred to as the *Rivière de Morlaix* (the Morlaix River). The town itself squeezes on to

Left: Apostle sculpture in the church porch, Guimiliau

the river's banks, spreading up the steep slopes on either side. Built in 1863 the great railway viaduct — Morlaix's most distinctive landmark (59 m high and 284 m long) — spans the narrow valley, as does the curving modern bridge carrying the motorway. Morlaix is one of north Brittany's busiest trade and shopping centres although the port which flourished in the Middle Ages is nowadays used mainly by pleasure craft.

 A walk among half-timbered houses
Several of the streets which crowd into the valley bottom are packed with medieval half-timbered houses with projecting upper storeys. All repay a visit but those in the Grand' Rue are particularly attractive. Equally famous among Morlaix's buildings is the *Maison de la*

Morlaix

Duchesse, a 16th c. house in the Rue du Mûr which once belonged to the Duchess Anne. The former *Jacobin church* is now a museum of folk art and modern paintings.

   Boatyard; boats for hire.

Le Meur, 11 Place des Otages: crêperie; *Le Cheval d'orgueil*, 49 Rue du Mûr: fish dishes, unusual murals of nautical scenes; *La Table de Rabelais*, 9 Rue du Fil; *Auberge des Gourmets*, 90 Rue Gambetta.

The coast north of Morlaix
On the Kernéléhen peninsula north of Morlaix, not far from Plouézoch, stands the great *Barnenez* tumulus, the most important megalithic burial site in northern Brittany. Dating from between 4000 and 3600 BC it has eleven burial chambers beneath an earth mound. Between the Pointe de Diben and the Pointe de Primel lie a series of sandy beaches divided by rocky headlands.

Boats are available for hire at *Plougasnou*, a small seaside resort. At *Locquirec,* a fishing village and holiday resort with facilities for thalassotherapy, the church boasts a Renaissance tower and an interesting 16th c. altarpiece. And at *Lanmeur*, within an otherwise modern church is to be found the oldest surviving ecclesiastical building in Brittany, an Early Romanesque crypt.

From Morlaix drive north-west to the little seaside resort of *Carantec*. The *Chaise du Curé* (Parson's chair) provides a lovely view down over the Baie de Morlaix. Offshore lie two islands, Taureau, with a château, and Callot.

St-Pol-de-Léon Pop. 8,000
St-Pol-de-Léon, named after St Pol the Aurelian, a Welsh missionary, was the first bishopric to be created in Brittany.

Roscoff harbour

It has two quite exceptional architectural attractions. The first is the great 77-m-high belfry towering above the transept of the Kreisker Chapel (14th and 15th c.), the model for many a Breton bell-tower. The second is the beautifully proportioned Gothic cathedral (13th and 16th c.). A wealth of figures decorate the superbly carved choir-stalls (1512) on which the artist has depicted scenes from St Pol's life.

 Boats for hire.

Roscoff Pop. 3,800

This much visited seaside resort and centre for marine research is also a fishing port with a yacht harbour and a commercial dock specialising in the shipment of early vegetables. Its Gothic church of *Notre-Dame-de-Kroaz-Baz* and the Renaissance-style round tower by the harbour are both interesting. The *Charles Pérez* aquarium has an exhibition of native species of fish. There could be no better advertisement for the mild climate of the north Breton coast than the great fig-tree in the inner courtyard of no. 6 Rue des Capucins. It was planted by monks in 1621.

From the modern ferry terminal there are services to England (Plymouth) and Eire (Cork) carrying the many tourists who come to this area from the UK and Ireland.

Boats for the *Île de Batz* (no cars) leave from the old harbour. The island, 1.5 km wide and 3.5 km long, is virtually treeless but has a harbour (tidal) and some delightful beaches. The panorama from the 41-m-high lighthouse is rewarding too.

Le Val-André

Côtes-du-Nord: sand, bays and granite cliffs

The department of Côtes-du-Nord extends 250 km along the Channel coast. Following one upon the other from east to west come the Côte d'Emeraude, Côte de Penthièvre, Côte du Goëlo and Côte de Granit Rose, the last being exceptionally beautiful with an abundance of fascinating rock formations. The coastal landscape is one of cliffs, seemingly endless beaches, colourful little harbours, and seaside villages. Behind them lies a green hinterland of woods and heathland, ploughed fields, streams – teeming with fish – and lakes. The popular Lake Guerlédan has excellent facilities for bathing, sailing, windsurfing, rowing and canoeing.

St-Brieuc Pop. 56,000

St-Brieuc, administrative capital of the department, lies on the bay of the same name. It is a commercial and industrial centre with some important markets and an annual trade fair, and the commercial port and fishing harbour also play a big role in the city's economy.

St-Brieuc occupies a favoured site on a plateau intersected by the valleys of the Rivers Gouëdic and Gouët, both crossed by impressive viaducts. With its picturesque Old Town around the Place de la Grille the city is much frequented by holidaymakers.

 Sightseeing in St-Brieuc

The striking, fortress-like 12th–14th c. cathedral of *St-Etienne* was erected over the burial place of the missionary Brieuc. Two square towers of differing heights and with loopholes and machicolations flank the façade of a building which embodies every style from Gothic through Renaissance to Rococo.

The *Musée d'Histoire des Côtes-du-Nord* in the Rue des Lycéens-Martyrs includes sections on the department's social and environmental history.

A fine view of the canalised River Gouët is gained from the *Tertre Aubé*, a hill in the north-east of the city, while the *Rond Point Huguin* in the east overlooks the River Gouëdic.

 Archery, kite-flying.

 Outings on the unspoilt coast

From immediately north-east of St-Brieuc to the *Pointe du Roselier* spectacular cliffs provide fine views of the bay. Further east, birdwatchers will enjoy the *Anse* (bay) *d'Yffiniac,* a publicly owned bird sanctuary (sandpiper, stint and greenshank).

The coast between St-Brieuc and Dinard
The Baie de St-Brieuc

Both sides of the Baie de St-Brieuc are strung with resorts, some large and some small. All can lay claim to sandy beaches, though the smaller ones on the western side – the more rugged of the two – often lie in narrow little bays encircled by steep cliffs. Despite the attractions of its tiny, thoroughly charming villages the strip of coast between St-Brieuc and Le Val-André seems almost undiscovered by tourists.

Le Val-André to Sables-d'Or-les-Pins

Le Val-André with its glorious sandy beaches is a popular resort. Some 4.5

km beyond it a road branches off right to *Bienassis,* a 15th and 16th c. château set in a lovely park (open to the public). At *Erquy* (pop. 3,300), another small holiday resort, scallop-fishing brings a real bustle to the little harbour. True to its name, *Sables-d'Or-les-Pins* is a mixture of pine woods and sandy beaches. It also has a casino.

Inland to Lamballe

A visit to this small country town (pop. 5,500) about 16 km inland is sure to appeal to anyone who loves horses. Lamballe is the home of a famous stud founded in 1825 which today maintains over a hundred stallions. In the town itself old houses still line the *Place du Martrai*, while the *Maison du Bourreau* (Executioner's House) contains two museums, one dedicated to the painter Mathurin Meheut (a native of Lamballe), the other the town's history museum. The 12th c. collegiate church of *Notre-Dame* is predominantly Gothic but with one or two Romanesque elements, for example in the porch. Note the carved wooden rood screen.

Cap Fréhel

For about 9 km beyond Sables-d'Or-les-Pins a lovely coast road winds its way towards this magnificent headland. It is a gaunt, 70-m-high plateau of rock which drops away precipitously to the sea to be buffeted almost incessantly by huge breakers. A stubborn carpet of heather and yellow gorse clings to the patches of slate and sandstone spared by wind and weather. A breathtaking panorama extends from Pointe du Grouin in the east all the way round to the Île de Bréhat in the west. The lighthouse can be visited. Cap Fréhel is also a well-known bird sanctuary alive with cormorants and shags, guillemots, kitti-wakes and herring gulls. From August

onwards it becomes a staging post for birds on their southward migration: gannets, scoters, terns, manx shearwaters, and many others.

A short drive south-east of Cap Fréhel stands the 13th and 14th c. stronghold *Fort la Latte*. It perches 60 m above the sea, complete with drawbridge, ramparts and massive fortified towers (private property, but with guided tours).

West of Dinard

St-Cast-le-Guildo (pop. 3,000) is situated on a headland of the same name. There are good sandy beaches, and well-marked cliff paths to the Pointe de St-Cast and the Pointe de la Garde, from both of which fine views of the Emerald Coast can be obtained. Then comes *St-Jacut-de-la-Mer*, with its extensive oyster- and mussel-beds, followed by *Lancieux* and *St-Briac-sur-Mer*, two more small resorts with fishing and yacht harbours.

West of St-Brieuc

The delightful little resorts on the west side of the Baie de St-Brieuc (St-Laurent-de-la-Mer, Les Rosaires, Binic, Etables-sur-Mer and – best known of all – St-Quay-Portrieux) are all very well endowed, having seawater swimming pools and facilities for a variety of sports.

Just a little way inland *Kermaria-an-Isquit* (the name means 'place of Mary who heals') is famous for its pilgrim chapel. Frescos (15th c.) including one depicting a Dance of Death are among the chapel's fine examples of traditional Breton art.

Beyond Kermaria (on the D21) the

Abbaye de Beauport

tiny village of *Lanleff* contains a real curiosity, a ruined Romanesque temple in the form of a rotunda. The twelve inner arches survive more or less intact. At Kérity a few kilometres south-east of Paimpol a road leads off left (coastwards) to the 13th and 14th c. *Abbaye de Beauport*, formerly a house of the Premonstratensian order, complete with vaulted Gothic cider cellar. The picturesque ruin makes a worthwhile outing.

The Côte de Granit Rose

Between Paimpol and Trébeurden is found one of the most spectacular stretches of coastline in Brittany, the Côte de Granit Rose, so called on account of the colour of its rock. Massive granite formations abound, huge natural edifices steeped in legend and given aptly evocative names such as *Château du Diable*.

News courtesy of space

France's satellite telecommunications station (Le Centre de Télécommunication par Satellite) is located here in the department of Côtes-du-Nord, at Pleumeur-Bodou about 8 km north-west of Lannion. It was established in 1962 in response to the rapid progress being made in satellite communications technology and the ever increasing demand for world-wide telecommunications services. Since then it has been constantly updated to keep abreast of technological innovation. Rising above the green landscape is a huge white sphere, the radar dome (64 m in diameter and 50 m high), beneath which is a large horn antenna. The Centre handles intercontinental telephone and television transmissions through a system of six substations. The differing designs of each sub-station's wide-surface antennae reflect the level of technological development at the time of construction. The parabolic antennae are accurate to within a few hundredths of a degree and are virtually immune to interference. Every instrument is kept under constant surveillance with on-screen monitoring and automatic data recording. For all the technological sophistication the underlying principle of satellite telecommunications is extremely simple. A signal transmitted from one earth station is picked up by the satellite and relayed down to a receiving station somewhere else on the globe.

Paimpol Pop. 8,500

Paimpol's harbour, once used by the men who fished Icelandic waters, is now the home port of a mainly coastal fishing fleet. The town makes its living chiefly by cultivating oysters and growing early vegetables. It became well known far beyond the frontiers of Brittany when Pierre Loti made it the setting for his novel *Pêcheurs d'Islande*.

The scenery of the *Pointe de l'Arcouest* is exceptionally beautiful; the headland is fringed with islands, rocky islets and reefs. Crossings from Arcouest to the Île de Bréhat take ten minutes.

Île de Bréhat

The Île is 3.5 km long, 1.5 km wide and home to a mere 550 people. It is kept free of cars, tractors being the only means of motor transport. Visitors are attracted by the pretty footpaths and delightful beaches, and Mediterranean plants thrive in the mild climate. Many a poet and painter has found inspiration on this island of flowers.

Tréguier Pop. 3,700

Its people having been converted to Christianity by St Tugdual in the 6th c., Tréguier became one of Brittany's early bishoprics. The town lies spread over a terraced hillside. The cathedral of *St-Tugdual* (13th–15th c.) is one of the region's most elaborate Gothic churches. Among its impressive features are the three towers over the transept, one with a delicately pierced Gothic spire. The Late Gothic cloister with its Flamboyant arcades, the choir-stalls and the fine stained-glass windows also merit attention. A short distance from the cathedral, on the shady *Place du Martray*, is a monument to the philosopher-theologian Ernest Renan (1823–92); the author of the *Histoire des Origines du Christianisme* was born in Tréguier. The house at 20 Rue Renan

The Côte de Granit Rose near Ploumanach

is now a museum dedicated to him.

Ex **A short drive north and west**
Seven kilometres north of Tréguier on the D8 stands the chapel of St-Gonéry (15th and 16th c.), its timber vaulting decorated with naïve paintings. The *Pointe du Château* headland and tiny harbour of Pors-Hir are 3.5 km further on. From there head south-west to the quaint fishing village of *Port-Blanc* with its unusual chapel of Notre-Dame (16th c.) and calvary.

Perros-Guirec Pop. 8,000
This popular seaside town has splendid beaches, a fishing and yacht harbour, and an interesting 12th c. pink granite church, *St-Jacques-le-Majeur*. There are boat trips to Les Sept-Îles (bird sanctuary) and a ferry service to Jersey and Guernsey in the Channel Islands.

   Thalassotherapy.

Des Rochers, Port de Ploumanach: fish dishes; *France*, 4 Rue Rouzig: lovely view.

Trébeurden

Corniche Bretonne

From Perros-Guirec via Trégastel-Plage to Trébeurden runs the Corniche Bretonne, a highly scenic coastal road commanding a wealth of lovely views. Along the way the two small resorts of *Plou-manach* and *Trégastel-Plage* vie with one another in the extraordinary variety of shapes to be seen among their astonishing giant granite rocks. Both also have lovely beaches.

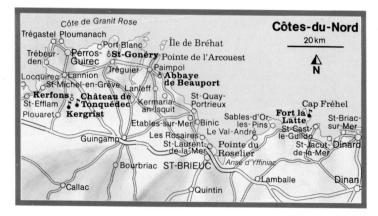

Marine aquarium.

 There is a most inviting cliff-top walk from Perros-Guirec to Ploumanach following what is known as the Sentier des Douaniers (Customs Officers' Path). Further along the Corniche Bretonne in the direction of Trébeurden there is a turn-off to the right leading to the *Île Grande*, where there are megalithic monuments to be seen.

Trébeurden Pop. 3,000

Trébeurden, most westerly of the resorts on the Côte de Granit Rose, is quieter than the others though it does have several beaches. From *Bihit* and *Le Castel*, two small headlands nearby, there are lovely views seawards and over the islands offshore. At low water you can walk across to the island of *Milliau* (dolmen) – a thoroughly enjoyable excursion.

Next on the itinerary comes Lannion, best reached by driving back in the direction of Trégastel and turning right at the junction of the D788 and D21. Just through Penvern a road leads off to the famous 5-m-high Christianised *St-Duzec* menhir. Christian symbols and figures have been carved into the stone – Christianity victorious over the forces of paganism.

Lannion Pop. 18,000

This lively provincial town with its busy port, developing industries and high-rise buildings has nevertheless managed to preserve its Old Town, on a hill above the River Léguer. Here you can find old

The coast at Lannion

Lannion

half-timbered houses with projecting upper storeys and slate roofs. Some are decorated with caryatids – carved female figures supporting the framework. A visit to *Brélévenez* church, built by the Templars in the 12th c., means a long climb up 142 granite steps, but it is worth the effort just to admire the stupendous view over the town.

Ex Exploring the coast

Take the D786 to the little beach resort of *St-Michel-en-Grève*. Between St-Michel and the tiny village of St-Efflam is the *Grand Rocher*, an 80-m-high vantage-point. Beyond St-Efflam the *Corniche de l'Armorique* runs along the coast as far as Locquirec providing a delightful and very varied drive. Locquirec itself is a small resort and fishing port with a yacht harbour, lovely sandy beaches and dunes.

Inland from Lannion

From Lannion follow the D11 for about 7 km in the direction of Plouaret before branching off left to *Kergrist Château* (14th and 17th c. façades). Rejoin the D11 and head back towards Lannion, turning right after just half a kilometre for the 15th and 16th c. *Kerfons* chapel (about 2 km on side-roads). Of special interest here is the carved wooden rood screen. Return along the same route for about 1 km where a road off to the left leads next to the ruined castle of *Tonquédec* on the banks of the Léguer. Built in the 13th c. the castle was pulled down in the 17th c. Equally romantic in its setting is the ruined *Coatfrec* castle a few kilometres to the north.

Guingamp Pop. 10,800

Guingamp, further inland, is an important agricultural centre. New industries are also establishing themselves in the town, which is advantageously sited at a vital intersection between the fast N12/E50 and several other roads. The Renaissance fountain in Guincamp is famous; it is beautifully carved and has three basins, one in lead and two in stone. Famous too is the Black Virgin statue in the Gothic church of *Notre-Dame-de-Bon-Secours* (14th c.). A torchlight procession is held in her honour on the Saturday before the first Sunday in July. Fragments of the town's feudal ramparts have been preserved, as have some old half-timbered and granite houses.

 Le Relais du Roi, 42 Place du Centre: fish.

Mont-St-Michel

Mont-St-Michel: pyramid in the sea

Mont-St-Michel is almost always crowded. Most visitors prefer to drive over on the causeway rather than follow the example of the 'miquelots' or pilgrims of days gone by and make the crossing on foot. Then as now the rocky island had to be reached from the southern shore of the bay; picking their way across the ever dangerous tidal mud-flats through water-filled channels and pools, the pilgrims would struggle over sand-banks and mussel-beds, sometimes having to hurry to safety just ahead of the incoming tide.

The difference in sea-level between high and low water here is 14 m, turning Mont-St-Michel into an island on the flood. It once belonged to Brittany. But the deposition of sediments by the River Couesnon and the consequent westward displacement of the river's course (and with it the border between the ancient duchies) meant that the holy shrine was lost to Normandy. The silting up continues even today, and could put Mont-St-Michel's attractive island setting at risk.

The abbey sits ensconced on its 78-m-high granite cone, silhouetted like a pyramid against the sea. Buttressing walls had to be built right from the base of the rock to provide support for the foundations. Above these rise several storeys of thick-walled crypts, abbey buildings and outbuildings, all topped by the slender Gothic spire of the abbey church. This is crowned in turn by a statue of the Archangel, whose outstretched wings seem to touch the sky. It is an extraordinary and quite magnificent sight.

Mont-St-Michel

 A brief history

In 704 the Archangel Michael appeared to the Bishop of Avranches, charging him with the building of a church on Mont Tombe (as the mount was then known). From this the splendour that is now 'St Michael's Mount' developed over the centuries. There were three distinct architectural phases. The first, the pre- and Early Romanesque phase,

came in the 10th and 11th c. with the building of a Late Carolingian-style church, Notre-Dame-sous-Terre. In 1060 the Norman Duke Richard I established a Benedictine abbey here and the pre-Romanesque building was incorporated as a crypt into a new Romanesque abbey church. Monastic buildings were also erected on the side of the mount. The Romanesque second phase was carried out in the 12th c. under the English kings, and was followed in the 13th c. by the Gothic third phase at a time when the French kings had once again acquired control. From this third period date the Merveille buildings with their Guests' and Pilgrims' Halls, storerooms, refectory, Knights' Hall, dormitories, cloister, abbot's lodge and ramparts around the Châtelet.

📷 Tour of the pilgrims' mount

As early as the 14th c. this holy place attracted some 15,000 pilgrims a year. Nowadays in the summer months 6,000 people a day come here. Crowds jostle their way through the only entrance, the *Porte de l'Avancée*, and along the solitary street of the tiny little town below the abbey, the *Grande Rue*, lined with a plethora of souvenir shops, antique-shops, restaurants, cafés, crêperies and hotels.

To visit the abbey itself you must join one of the 45-minute guided tours (English-speaking guide). You are taken through a labyrinth of passages, staircases and vaults, proceeding by storey rather than according to architectural style. Afterwards you emerge into the open of the abbey garden. There are two museums tracing the history of Mont-St-Michel, the *Musée Historique* and the *Musée Historial du Mont*. Both have displays of wax figures; the second also makes use of slides and photos.

Useful things to know

Before you go
Climate and when to go

Brittany has a maritime climate with mild winters, moderately warm summers, and a fair amount of rain at all times of the year. The influence of the Gulf Stream means that even in winter frosty spells are exceedingly rare. Westerly winds bring moist air masses from the Atlantic which pass quickly inland until they meet the higher ground, where the moisture is released as rain (Monts d'Arrée 1,500 mm, St-Malo 700 mm a year). In the coastal areas there is constant change from clear skies to showers. Long periods of fine weather can be expected only in high summer (the average temperature in July is 18°C).

Brittany is very crowded in July and August (the peak of the French holiday season) and accommodation must then be booked in advance. But by the same token there is always a vast choice in the fields of entertainment, sport and other amenities available during this period.

Insurance

You are strongly advised to take out holiday insurance, including cover against medical expenses.

As a member of the EC France has a reciprocal agreement with other EC countries, under which free medical treatment can be obtained for those entitled to it in their own country. To obtain this benefit a UK national has to be in possession of form E111, obtainable from the DSS; an application form is available from the DSS or at main post offices.

Anyone travelling by car should arrange comprehensive insurance cover for the duration of the holiday.

Getting to Brittany

By sea: For British visitors Brittany is easily reached via the western and central channel ports (for example Plymouth–Roscoff or Portsmouth–St-Malo).

By rail: Nowadays Brittany is no longer the isolated peninsula it was until relatively recent times. All the major towns and cities can be reached by rail from Paris (Gare Montparnasse).

By air: All the major international airlines of course fly to Paris, but there are also a number of airports in Brittany (for example at Rennes, Brest and Quimper) as well as at Nantes to which there are regular internal flights from Paris and other cities.

Passport and customs regulations

No visa required by British or US visitors staying under three months. British tourists need a valid standard passport or British Visitor's Passport.

Personal belongings of people entering the country are not subject to duty. These include still and video cameras, tape recorders, portable radios, telescopes and binoculars, portable typewriters and the usual camping equipment. In addition, EC residents may bring in (duty paid) 300 cigarettes (or 75 cigars or 400 g tobacco), 5 litres of wine and 1.5 litres of spirits over 22% (3 litres under 22%).

EC residents may take into or bring back from France duty free 200 cigarettes or 50 cigars or 250 g tobacco, 1 litre of spirits over 22% (2 litres under 22%) and 2 litres of wine.

Non-EC visitors should check allowances with their travel agent.

During your stay

Currency

The monetary unit in France is the French franc (F), equivalent to 100 centimes (c). Currently in circulation are coins up to the value of 10 F as well as banknotes in denominations of 10, 20, 50, 100 and 500 F. Exchange rates are subject to fluctuation and should be checked in the national press or at banks.

There are no restrictions on the import of foreign currency into France. All French banks, bureaux de change and most hotels will cash Eurocheques.

Credit cards are in fairly common use; most hotels, restaurants and petrol stations and many shops will accept the major ones. However, it is safest to carry a supply of cash with you against the possibility of their not being accepted.

Accommodation

Hotels: There are hotels of every category (two-star hotels offer rooms with bath or shower and are perfectly satisfactory). The 'Logis et Auberges de France' (identified by a green sign with yellow fireplace) are good traditional hotels providing regional cooking and an informal atmosphere.

Holiday cottages (Gîtes Ruraux) are common on farms and in villages, though seldom beside the sea (information from the Fédération Nationale des Gîtes Ruraux de France, 35 Rue Godot de Mauroy, 75009 Paris). Other holiday homes (*meublées,* studios, apartments) are available virtually everywhere. Prices vary greatly depending on comfort, size and location.

Gîtes d'Etapes are similar to youth hostels and offer plain accommodation for hikers and cyclists (information from A.B.R.I., 3 Rue des Portes Mordelaises,

35000 Rennes).

Youth hostels (Auberges de Jeunesse) provide facilities for cooking, as well as sailing and windsurfing instruction, bicycle hire and sometimes camping (information from the Fédération Unie des Auberges de Jeunesse, 6 Rue Mesnil, 75116 Paris).

Camping: Campsites (usually with 100 to 200 places) are concentrated along the coast and inland near villages and small towns of particular interest to tourists. They range from extremely comfortable and expensive sites with swimming pools and tennis courts to cheap basic sites. In the peak season (July/August) they tend to be very crowded and it is essential to book if you are intending to stay for any length of time.

Many hotels and almost all campsites are closed out of season from October to May. The often reasonably priced holiday homes and flats on the other hand are usually available throughout the year. Local tourist offices keep registers of accommodation from which you can discover whether a hotel, holiday home or campsite is open.

Events in the calendar

Festivals and pardons are held all over Brittany, chiefly in the summer months. The most noteworthy are as follows.

Festivals

3rd Sunday in May: *Combourg* flower festival. Whit Monday: Grand Festival at *Toulfouën.* 3rd Sunday in June: strawberry festival in *Plougastel-Daoulas.* 2nd Sunday in July: embroiderers' festival in *Pont-l'Abbé.* 3rd Sunday in July: seagull festival in *Douarnenez*; apple-tree festival in *Fouesnant*; castle festival in *Plomelin*; carnation festival in *St-Malo-*

Paramé. 4th Sunday in July: Grand Festival of Cornouaille in *Quimper*. 1st Sunday in August: international bagpipe festival in *Brest*. 2nd Saturday and Sunday in August: Grand Festival in *Morlaix*. 2nd Sunday in August: cormorant festival in *Penmarch*. 3rd Sunday in August: Breiz-Rosko festival in *Roscoff*; Grand Pilgrimage in *La Baule*. Penultimate Sunday in August: Festival of the Blue Nets in *Concarneau*. 2nd Sunday in September: festival in *St-Brieuc*. 4th Sunday in September: wind-instrument pardon in *Gourin*.

Pardons

Sunday nearest to May 19th: Tréguier, Pilgrimage of St Yves, patron saint of lawyers. 2nd Sunday in July: Troménie in *Locronan;* Grande Troménie every six years (1995, 2001). July 25th and 26th: St Anne's Pardon at *Ste-Anne-d'Auray*. August 15th: Grand Pardon of Notre-Dame in *Rumengol*; Pardon of Notre-Dame-de-Roscuden in *Pont-Croix*; Notre-Dame Pardon in *Perros-Guirec*. Last Sunday in August: Pardon of Notre-Dame in *Le Folgoët*; Pardon of *Ste-Anne-la-Palud*. September 8th: Pardon of Notre-Dame-du-Roncier in *Josselin*.

Help in an emergency

Chemists and medical treatment: Chemists' shops (*pharmacies*) have a sign bearing a large green cross. The chemist will supply the address of the nearest doctor or dentist on call as well as of hospitals with casualty departments. Many chemists' shops and private surgeries (*médecin, docteur*) are closed on Mondays. Treatment must be paid for on the spot.

Emergency telephone numbers
Police: 17; fire: 18.

Opening times

Administrative departments with offices open to the public: 9 am–noon.

Banks: Mondays to Fridays 9 am–noon, 2–4 pm, Saturdays 9 am–noon.

Châteaux: Opening times vary considerably. Most are open between spring and autumn.

Churches and abbeys: Normally closed between noon and 2 pm.

Museums: Larger state-owned museums are usually open on Sundays (when entrance is free); privately owned museums on the other hand are normally closed on Sundays. During the week most museums close on either Monday or Tuesday.

Shops: Larger shops in the towns are open from 9.30 am to 6.30 pm; others shut for lunch between 1 and 4 pm. Food shops are usually open on Sunday mornings, but most are closed on Mondays.

Post and telephone

Post offices (*PTT*) are open from Mon. to Fri., 8 am–12 noon and 2–6 pm, Sat. from 8 am–12 noon. Stamps *(timbres)* are also available from tobacconists' shops. Remember when posting letters that one box is for the *département* you are in while the other, marked 'autres destinations', is for mail addressed abroad or to other parts of France.

Public telephones are identified by a black and yellow disc-shaped sign. Telephone cards, obtainable from post offices and *bars tabacs*, are widely used. Direct dialling abroad is possible from all telephone kiosks. When making a call abroad first dial the international service number (19) and wait for the tone before dialling the code (44 for the UK, 1 for the US and Canada; omit initial 0 from the area code). International calls are comparatively cheap, though hotels impose a surcharge of about 50%.

Public holidays

New Year: January 1st
Easter Monday
Labour Day: May 1st
Armistice Day (1945): May 8th
Ascension Day
Whit Monday
National holiday (Bastille Day): July 14th
Feast of the Assumption: August 15th
All Saints' Day: November 1st
Armistice Day (1918): November 11th
Christmas: December 25th

Leisure activities

Bathing: The bathing season on the Breton coast lasts from June to October. It is still possible to find magnificent beaches which are relatively unfrequented. If planning to swim from an unfamiliar or isolated beach, first ask someone with local knowledge about possible currents and keep a look out for notices banning bathing. The speed with which the tide comes in can be a real danger, even to strong swimmers (tide tables are available from the *Syndicats d'Initiative* – see page 92). If you witness a seaside accident of any sort report it at once to the nearest Quartier des Affaires Maritimes or Centre Régional de Surveillance et de Sauvetage.

Canal and river holidays: Various hire-boats to suit every requirement are available from some twenty centres. All the larger boats are fully equipped with cooking facilities, heating and sanitation. No permit is required to handle the boats, which are virtually unsinkable and cannot be driven above 6 kph. There are about 600 km of waterways inviting leisurely exploration – the only obstacles to be faced in Brittany are the locks (information from the Comité de Promotion Touristique des Canaux Bretons, 3 Rue des Portes Mordelaises, 35000 Rennes).

Cycling is enormously popular in France and bicycles can be hired almost anywhere in Brittany. Although cycle tracks are few and far between, side-roads are quiet and seldom dangerous, and offer a wonderful way to experience the countryside.

Horse-drawn caravans: The caravans (*roulottes*) are self-catering (gas cookers, crockery, bedding). The holiday-maker is responsible for feeding and harnessing the horse. Stopping places near villages (information from the *Syndicats d'Initiative*).

Thalassotherapy: Spas, iodine-rich air, salt water, the maritime climate, massage, hydrotherapy, sun-lamps, algae and stress therapy – all this and much more is available for the treatment of such conditions as rheumatism, arthritis and exhaustion. Brittany's eight hydrotherapy centres are run in conjunction with luxury hotels and 'diet' food restaurants (information is available from tourist offices).

Walking: The Maison de la Randonnée ABR (Association Bretonne des Relais et Itinéraires), 9 Rue des Portes Mordelaises, 35000 Rennes, can supply maps suitable for walkers. A guide to the long-distance paths through Brittany is also available.

Watersports: Information on all watersports can be obtained from the Comité Régional de Tourisme, 1 Rue Poullain-Duparc, 35000 Rennes.

Touring by car

Vehicles travel on the right. Seat belts must be worn at all times. Motorists should carry the following: a nationality plate fixed to the back of the car; a warning triangle (unless car has hazard lights); spare sets of bulbs for all lights.

Priority: The old system, whereby traffic entering a road from the right had priority (*priorité à droite*), no longer applies, traffic on major roads now having priority (as does traffic already on roundabouts). However, signs will occasionally indicate exceptions (for example at some roundabouts) and drivers should familiarise themselves with these signs.

Speed limits: in built-up areas 50 kph (31 mph); outside built-up areas 90 kph (56 mph), but 80 kph (50 mph) in rain; on dual carriageways 110 kph (68 mph), but 100 kph (62 mph) in rain; on motorways 130 kph (81 mph), but 110 kph (68 mph) in rain. Drivers who have held a licence for less than one year: 90 kph maximum.

Documents: In addition to a valid driving licence and vehicle registration certificate it is advisable for motorists to obtain an international 'green card' insurance certificate.

Filling stations in country areas are often few and far between, or so modestly equipped that it is easy to miss them. Many close at lunch-time. Stations selling lead-free petrol (*essence sans plomb*) can be found in most towns and on motorways.

Electricity
220 v/50 Hz AC. French sockets do not normally take the standard UK or US plug; a Continental adaptor (obtainable from electrical dealers) will almost certainly be necessary.

Binoculars
A pair of binoculars is really essential, not just for watching wildlife in the nature reserves but also for seeing the detail of the high-level carvings and frescos which embellish many of the churches.

Tipping
A service charge (*service compris* or *s.c.*) is included by law in France in all hotels and restaurants. It is customary to round small amounts upwards but not to give an additional tip.

Maps and books
RAC Atlas France has clear detailed up-to-date mapping for the motorist at the scale of 1:250,000 (approx. 4 miles to 1 inch). Covers the whole of France plus Belgium and Luxembourg.

RAC Regional Map of Brittany, also at a scale of 1:250,000 (approx. 4 miles to 1 inch). An invaluable sheet map for visitors to the region with tourist information and full road details.

RAC Gault-Millau The Best of France English version of this witty and authoritative guide to the best restaurants and hotels in France.

Important addresses
Diplomatic offices
British Embassy
35 Rue du Faubourg St-Honoré
75008 Paris; tel. 1 42 66 91 42

US Embassy
2 Av Gabriel
75008 Paris; tel. 1 42 96 12 02

Canadian Embassy
35 Av Montaigne
75008 Paris; tel. 1 47 23 01 01

Australian Embassy
4 Rue Jean Rey
75724 Paris; tel. 1 45 75 62 00

New Zealand Embassy
7 ter Rue Léonard de Vinci
75116 Paris; tel. 1 45 00 24 11

Irish Embassy
4 Rue Rude
75116 Paris; tel. 1 45 00 20 87

Tourist information

In UK

French Government Tourist Office
178 Piccadilly
London WIV OAL; tel. 071 499 6911

French Railways
179 Piccadilly
London W1V OBA; tel. 071 493 4451

In USA

French Government Tourist Office
610 Fifth Avenue
New York NYC 10021

In France

Larger towns and smaller ones with tourist interest have a *Syndicat d'Initiative* (tourist office). Here you will find an abundance of brochures about anything and everything, from tourist routes to restaurants, hotels and festivals, regional museums and nature parks, the town itself, the surrounding area and the whole *département*. Many hotels also keep a supply of tourist information.

RAC

RAC Motoring Services Ltd
RAC House
PO Box 100
South Croydon CR2 6XW;
tel. 081 686 2525

French national motoring organisations

Automobile Club de France
6–8 Place de la Concorde
75008 Paris; tel. 1 42 65 34 70

Association Française des Automobilistes
9 Rue Anatole de la Forge
75017 Paris; tel. 1 42 27 82 00

Breton farm building

Useful words and phrases

Although English is fairly widely understood in established tourist areas, the visitor will undoubtedly find a few words and phrases of French very useful.

please	s'il vous plaît
thank you (very much)	merci (bien)
yes/no	oui/non
excuse me	pardon
do you speak English?	parlez-vous anglais?
I do not understand	je ne comprends pas
good morning	bonjour
good evening	bonsoir
good night	bonne nuit
goodbye	au revoir
how much?	combien?
I should like	je voudrais
a room with private bath	une chambre avec bain
the bill, please! (in hotel)	la note, s'il vous plaît
(in restaurant)	l'addition
everything included	tout compris
when?	à quelle heure?
open	ouvert
shut	fermé
where is . . . street?	où se trouve la rue . . . ?
the road to . . . ?	la route de . . . ?
how far is it to . . . ?	quelle est la distance à . . . ?
to the left/right	à gauche/à droite
straight on	tout droit
post office	le bureau de poste
railway station	la gare
town hall	l'hôtel de ville/la mairie
exchange office	le bureau de change
police station	le commissariat/la poste de police
public telephone	la cabine téléphonique

tourist information office	l'office de tourisme/	0 zéro
	le syndicat d'initiative	1 un/une
doctor	le médecin	2 deux
chemist	le pharmacien	3 trois
toilet	la toilette	4 quatre
ladies	dames	5 cinq
gentlemen	messieurs	6 six
engaged	occupé	7 sept
free	libre	8 huit
entrance	l'entrée	9 neuf
exit	la sortie	10 dix
today/tomorrow	aujourd'hui/demain	11 onze
Sunday/Monday	dimanche/lundi	12 douze
Tuesday/Wednesday	mardi/mercredi	20 vingt
Thursday/Friday	jeudi/vendredi	50 cinquante
Saturday/holiday	samedi/jeu de congé	100 cent

Index

Original German text: Almut Rother. Translation: Wendy Bell
Series editor, English edition: Jane Rolph

© Verlag Robert Pfützner GmbH, München. Original German edition

© Jarrold Publishing, Norwich, Great Britain 1/91. English language edition worldwide

Published in the US and Canada by Hunter Publishing, Inc.,
300 Raritan Center Parkway, Edison NJ 08818

Illustrations: B. Bloomfield pages 15, 20 (left), 23 (top), 32, 43, 50 (both), 56 (left), 57 (both), 61 (top), 62 (bottom), 92; J. Allan Cash Ltd pages 54, 60; J. Davis Travel Photography pages 31, 38, 64; French Government Tourist Office pages 20 (right), 69; E. Greenwood page 49; P. Hall pages 3, 34 (both), 36, 46, 47, 61 (bottom, both), 66, 74, 79, 84; D. Hughes-Gilbey pages 1, 75; U. Snowdon page 86; World Pictures Ltd pages 12, 25, 41, 44, 52, 76, 78, 82

The publishers have made every endeavour to ensure the accuracy of this publication but can accept no responsibility for any errors or omissions. They would, however, appreciate notification of any inaccuracies to correct future editions.

Printed in Italy

ISBN 0–7117–0478–3